The Trip

A Modern Odyssey

Tom Sykes

Acknowledgements

Writing a book is a trying process, especially the first one. But writers are driven to do it as much as lemmings are driven to leap off of cliffs. This lemming has been a reluctant one however, but still a thorough lemming, who has been helped to the edge by others who have metaphorically gone before.

David Mook, poet, author, teacher, mentor and friend has been of exceptional help in this endeavor. His energy and enthusiasm through both the workshops he has originated and taught, and his dedication to the craft of writing have inspired the many beginners and veterans he has touched. His wit, experience, and encouragement has been a blessing.

Burnham Holmes, author, teacher, friend, writer of sonnets and veteran of countless editorial battles in skyscrapers far away, has brought guidance, advice, encouragement, and a lot of fun to the crafting and editing of these pages. Thank you Burnham.

Rebecca Gervais, designer, teacher, most helpful advocate, computer whiz, and number one daughter, has been of invaluable help in this project. Thank you Rebecca for your tireless support.

TOM SYKES

CONTENTS

Prologue

The Mechanic's Report

Friday

My auto mechanic told me,
My car was practically shot.
"Not worth fixing," he said,
"Transmission's grinding and the motor runs hot.
The muffler's too loud,
And the frame is all rusted.
The springs are sprung,
And the radio's busted."

"There's a leaking gasket somewhere,
That gives off an odor,
It's probably from the oil,
That's dripping down on the motor.
The clutch is slipping too,
And the oil pressure is low.
So when the red light comes on,
You'll have to drive slow."

"There's a crack in the windshield,
That distorted my view,
And the brake pads are worn right down,
Till they're blue.
The front end," he says.
"It's the alignment,
And it could get worse,
It's causing the tires to wear out,
And they're likely to burst."

"And the right rear tire," he said.
"Has a slow leak."
And he also noticed the spare,
"Was flat," when he took a peek.
"There's a funny noise in the back,
Maybe it's a bearing,
Or the differential's dry,
And the gears are wearing,"

"Anyway, the seals are leaking oil too,
But that's not causing the smell,
That's coming from the leak in the gas tank,"
Near as he could tell.
"The motor," he noted.
"Is running rough and stalls when she starts,
Probably needs new wires, spark plugs,
And some other fresh parts."

"But before we start in," he said.
"There's more you should know."
Now what? I thought.
What else has to go?
"There's a headlight out," he said.
"Maybe just a loose wire,
Or a bad bulb or a fuse,
But at least it hasn't caught fire."

"There's fleas in the back seat,
From your mangy old mutt,
And maybe ticks too!" he said,
As he slammed the door shut.
"There's a couple of springs here,
Sticking up in your seat.
What I said when I sat down there,
I best not repeat."

He said he could tape them over,
So I wouldn't rip my jeans,
But the tears in the headliner,
Were way beyond his means.
He figured the u-joints were loose too,
And the brakes needed bled,
Because the master cylinder was leaking too,
Well, that's what he said.

"You can keep the reservoir full,
If you add fluid every day,"
But how long till it fails,
He just couldn't say.
He adjusted the door,
So I didn't have to slam it so much,
But then the dome light came on,
When I pushed in the clutch.

"The warranty expired several years back."
I explained with a half shit-eating grin,
"And, well, the cost of repairs,
Will be too much to begin."
He shook his head
When I said it all would have to wait.
"At least," he said,
"Change the filter and fluids before it's too late."

I nodded in agreement,
As I looked up to speak,
"I'm driving cross country tomorrow, Joe.
But I'll bring it in next week."

Chapter One

Saturday

The next morning bright and early,
I started out on my trip.
At the second big hill,
The clutch started to slip,
Just like Joe said it would
If I tried to drive too fast.
So I slowed down to fifty five,
And hoped it would last.

I figured I had a long way to go,
From Memphis up to Cape Cod,
So I pulled into the granny lane,
Though it did feel kinda odd.
There I was crawling along,
Watching everybody fly past,
But the clutch stop slipping finally,
So I felt that she might last.

Things went along pretty uneventful after that,
Just real slow.
I-40's kind of straight and boring,
With not much to see and nowhere to go,
Unless you're looking for junk shops,
There's maybe ten at every exit.
I've stopped at plenty of them over the years,
But I don't suggest it.

By the time I got to Nashville,
I was low on fuel and hungry too.
After I got some gas I drove down town,
To see what was new.
I always liked the honkytonks,
With the music rolling right out into the streets.
I drove by my favorite, Roberts; it was early,
There might still be some seats.

I needed a break from the boredom,
And something to eat real soon.
There was a place to park in the shade out back,
By then it was already late afternoon.
The place was crowded,
But I found an empty stool at the bar.
I wanted to get something to take out quick,
That I could eat in the car.

But the bar maid said, "We quit serving food,
We only have beer on tap."
So I ordered a tall cold one with a fifty,
And a friendly little tip of my cap.
Five guys and a girl on the stage,
Were playing fiddles, guitars and a bass,
Singing an old George Jones song,
About lost love and a horse race.

Then came a Hank Williams song,
'Bout being lonely and blue,
Then a song about six days on the road,
And how I'm missing you.
The music was so good, I ordered another beer
When the first one got a little low.
The band kept on playing those great old tunes,
Some fast and some slow.

That steel guitar was whining;
Those boys could play pretty good.
So I sat there some more,
While they sang "Johnny B. Goode."
I was getting up to leave when they started singing,
"Please Release Me (Let Me Go)."
Why, I could have sat there all night drinking,
It was hard to say, "No."

I had a long way to go, but the magic gripped me,
So I grabbed one more quick shot,
Then I sat there in a trance, spell bound.
Man that "Orange Blossom Special" was hot.
Then the lady sang, "Walkin' After Midnight,"
Just like Patsy Cline at her best,
I knew I had to leave then,
Or drink alone and get all depressed.

I grabbed a half-pounder at the drive thru,
Before getting on the interstate,
With large fries, a piece of pie,
And a big vanilla milk shake.
As I pulled out on the highway,
Saying good bye to that old town,
I had to put on the headlights,
Cause the sun had gone down.

Those country tunes from the bar,
Were still playing in my head,
That's when I turned on the radio,
Before I remembered it was dead.
Nothing came out of it but a buzz;
It wouldn't even play a CD.
It made me mad to think
I hadn't had Joe fix it for me.

I finished the burger in silence,
And then the large fries and the pie.
That's when something really bright
In the rear view mirror caught my eye.
A bunch of flashing blue lights!
And the cop was flashing them at me, full blast.
What did I do this time? I thought.
I hadn't run a red light and I wasn't driving fast.

I sucked down my shake like a Hoover on high,
So he wouldn't smell the beer on my breath,
But when I rolled down the window I felt real hot,
Kind of like I was sweating to death.
"License and registration."
Was all that he said is a slow southern drawl.
I handed them over meekly,
Wondering what I had done and all.

I finished the shake kind of nervous,
While I watched him in my mirror.
It took him a long time there writing,
He was in no hurry that was clear.
He looked like a typical government worker of the day,
S L O W L Y earning his pay,
But finally he got out of the car
And I could see him waddling my way.

He handed back my license.
I stared at it, my eyes were kind of blurred.
"Do you know why I stopped you sir?" he asked.
This was a trick question I've often heard.
"You've got a headlight out," he finally announced.
"The law says that you need two."
He had some papers he was shuffling,
One pink and one blue.

He handed me the pink one, the carbon copy,
I could barely read what it said.
"I just gave you a warning this time,
But fix it in ten days or it's a ticket instead.
I noticed your car is smoking kind of bad too,
When I pulled you over for the headlight.
Maybe you ought to check the oil,
Something's just not right."

Then in summation he added,
As he looked over the top of the car,
"Boy son,
I hope you're not planning on going very far."
I guess I shook him up a little bit,
When I said "I'm heading to Cape Cod."
He stepped back a bit,
Then he mumbled, "Good God!"

He took another look at my inspection sticker,
Just to be sure of the date,
"Look," he said kind of seriously,
"It's getting pretty late.
You shouldn't be driving any longer.
With just one headlight.
There's a motel up ahead.
I think you ought to park it for the night."

Chapter Two

I didn't want to spend the money;
I was planning to drive right straight through.
But I got the hint and didn't argue
With cops the way I used to do.
"Is that an expensive place," I asked,
"That motel up ahead?"
"Not too bad Sir," he grinned,
"It'd be less than a ticket," he said.

I thanked him for his service,
The way every good citizen should do,
Then sat there and cursed very loudly,
As he disappeared into the blue.
When I finally cooled off and restarted the car,
The dome light stayed on,
But I covered it with duct tape,
And soon I was gone.

I was having trouble seeing the highway,
It might have been the beer or the one headlight,
Or looking through the cracked windshield.
It was a dark and moonless night.
But I was tired by then too,
And the whole sky had gotten dark.
Maybe the cop was right,
And it was a good time to park.

Up ahead I could make out some lights,
And then a sign on a low hill.
I remember thinking, Bates Motel, Bastille,
Or something from Amityville.
But it didn't look that bad;
The sign said "AC, adult movies, and cable TV."
There were a couple of semi's and a pickup,
Parked out front under a tree.

So I decided to make the best of it,
And pulled right on in.
I parked the car by the office,
And put on a big southern grin.
The night clerk was Pakistani or Indian,
Hard to understand but very polite.
I asked how he was doing and,
"Have you got a cheap room for the night?"

"Yes Sir," he said, "We have several nice rooms."
I could see he was trying to be shrewd.
"How much for your cheapest one?" I asked,
Not trying to seem rude.
"We have very nice room for one hundred dollar,"
He said, "You like, very fine."
That's when I noticed the cop had followed me,
And was parked out by the sign.

He only stayed a minute after the clerk waved his hand,
Then I paid the bill and got the key.
Lucky room number seven
Looked like a dump to me.
But of course the single bed was bigger
Than the back seat of my car,
But it was the smell of the mold and mildew,
That really gave me a jar.

Since the AC wasn't working,
I opened the window and let in some air,
Then I put my feet up on the table,
And tried to relax in the chair.
The room, I noticed, was pretty tiny,
Only about twelve feet each way.
But it was good enough, I told myself,
At least for a one night stay.

Bed, bathroom, wooden chair,
And a little table that held the TV.
It wasn't home but I could rest,
At least to some degree.
I washed my face in the tiny sink,
But the water never got hot.
I wasn't ready for a cold shower yet,
So I flopped down on the cot.

The remote didn't work at all,
But the TV came on with just a touch.
I searched for something to watch,
But there wasn't very much.
A lot of reruns, old movies,
And some fat hillbillies cutting down trees.
But that was better than all the channels,
In Spanish, or Portuguese.

Then there was all the religious networks,
Every one praying then asking for cash,
The weather for the week was rain coast to coast,
Then came the crash.
The whole set went black.
In a minute a sign came on that read,
"Pay clerk at office for more time,"
And that was all it said.

I was mad as hell and went back to the office,
And yelled at the clerk,
"Hey, buddy, what gives?
How come that crummy TV doesn't work?
You know your sign out there on the hill,
Says you got 'cable TV.'"
"Yes," he replied with his accent,
"But it does not say 'free.'"

"How much?" I asked,
My blood pressure was really rising,
"Five dollar please," he announced,
Then added after slightly pausing,
"But for ten you get player,
And three special DVD's."
He pointed to a shelf behind me on the wall,
It was sagging like a tired trapeze.

I stepped a little closer
To see what I could find,
Maybe a documentary or something silly,
So I could try to unwind.
But there was nothing like that there,
Search as I might;
Every movie was pornographic,
And most were in black and white.

Nearly all were foreign too,
With sub-titles and on a narrow little screen.
I glared at the clerk in growing disgust.
It was all so totally obscene.
"Are these the only movies you've got?
This stuff is just trash!"
"Yes. We have better ones in back,
But for twenty dollars more in cash."

He pointed to a curtain,
Over a door in the corner of the room,
I wasn't sold.
"They're the same porno crap, I presume?"
"Yes!" he said, "Only better.
You like, I make sure."
"No thanks," I said,
As I walked out and slammed the door.

The room was still musty,
When I went back inside,
By now it had started raining too,
So I had nowhere else to hide.
I decided to make the best,
Of the way that things had been cast.
I'd get a little sleep till morning,
Surely the worst was past.

Then I flopped on the bed,
And the springs gave out a squeak.
It was only a minute or two later on,
When the roof started to leak.
Just a drop or two on the pillow at first,
I easily rolled out of the way,
But the dripping kept getting worse;
Pretty soon it was practically a spray.

The bed was soon soaked like a sponge,
So I move over to the chair.
I also peeked out the window
To see if the manager was still there.
But the office light was out,
And of course the phone didn't work.
I sat in the dark fuming,
And thought about strangling that clerk.

But slowly I relaxed in the chair,
And my eyelids started to close down,
But every time I was nearly asleep,
I awoke to an unusual sound.
There was a guy's voice and then a girl's,
In the room right there next to mine,
And their bed springs had started squeaking too,
And they were a lot louder than mine.

They were trying to be quiet, at least that's what I thought
When I first awoke,
But a few minutes later, they talked more excited and louder,
That is whenever they spoke.
I smiled to myself,
At least there were some people still having fun.
After the springs finally quieted down,
I guessed they were done.

Chapter Three

I was nearly back to sleep again,
When I heard the woman quite clearly say,
"Ok Frank, get up and put your clothes back on,
Can't you see it's time for Ray?"
Then the bed springs started cranking again,
That familiar old grating tune.
It had rhythm and variation but it ended quickly
When Ray cried out real loud, "Oh June!"

But June didn't say anything in reply,
And things kind of quieted down,
Then the other guy yelled out,
"Come on, let's pour another round."
About that time another pickup truck
Arrived at their door.
Two big guys got out,
I expected they'd be cops for sure.

But then I heard Frank say,
"Hey Ray, look, Bobby and Sammy are here."
Then there was lots more laughing,
Apparently they'd brought more beer.
Well, it wasn't long after that,
Till the bed springs were squeaking again.
Then another truck arrived,
And two more guys came in.

There was more drinking and laughing,
And soon a poker game was going on,
But the bed springs never stopped squeaking,
At least not for very long.
So, between the all the noise next door,
And the water dripping on my bed,
It only made sense for me to go out
And sleep in my car instead.

I tilted the seat back and fell asleep in seconds
With the dome light under the duct tape still faintly on.
I woke up the next morning with a really stiff neck.
I was cold and kinked up, it was right after dawn.
The parking lot was empty by then,
All the trucks had left for town,
Everything was soaked with rain,
And it was still coming down.

Sunday

I was hungry and stiff as a board.
As I slowly climbed out of my car,
I felt a whole day had been wasted already,
I surely hadn't gotten far.
I went back in the room,
To clean up and wash my face,
I collected my things in my bag,
And was headed out of that place.

Just as I was closing the door,
I heard this sad little cry.
It was from inside the room next to mine.
It sounded more like a sob than a sigh.
Then I heard a meek voice call out, "mister."
It sounded more like a moan.
I turned as my neighbor's door opened slightly,
With a slow creaking groan.

A woman's face appeared at the door,
It was opened, but only a crack.
We stared at each other a moment;
I think we were both taken aback.
Slowly the door opened a little wider,
A tiny sleepy face was all I could see,
It was covered with blonde hair all uncombed,
Frizzy, flying and free.

"Mister," she said, she was wrapped up in a sheet.
"Could you help me out please?
I just need a ride a little bit up the road."
Then she started to sneeze.
But she had my attention when she continued again,
After slowly blowing her nose.
"My boyfriend left me here last night,
And I really hate to impose…"

I held up my hand in a motion for her to stop,
Her sad and mournful refrain,
Something inside me said, "get out of here man,
There's nothing you can gain,"
But then something else said,
"Wait a minute Bud, this isn't so bad,
Why not help the poor girl out.
Things look pretty sad."

After a moment of hesitation,
She continued where she had quit.
"I just need a short ride, Mister,
Only up the road a little bit."
She looked so helpless and bewildered,
She was clearly a damsel in distress.
How could I leave her all alone in her sheet,
Stranded at this dump and in such a mess?

"Ok," I said, "I've got some room.
I'll have to clear off the front seat."
"Oh, thank you Mister," she cried.
She sounded so tender and sweet.
"Hold on, I'll just be a minute please,
I've got to gather up some things in my bag."
But her "minute please" turned into ten or fifteen,
And the time was starting to drag.

At last the door opened again.
And she was standing there,
In really tight blue jeans and a wrinkled tee shirt,
But at least she'd combed her hair.
She actually looked pretty good to me,
There in the early morning light,
Considering, of course,
How busy she'd been all night.

I pushed open the door for her,
And she sat down right away.
As I drove the car out of the lot,
I was thinking of something to say,
But she spoke first and I had to smile,
It was just like in a cartoon.
She stretched out her hand and proudly said,
"Hi. My name is June."

Of course I had suspected just that,
But at first I didn't let on
"Glad to meet you June," I said as we shook.
"Everyone just calls me Don."
Her hand was nice and warm,
And it felt very soft to the touch,
Made me start to heat up inside,
Maybe a little too much.

"Where are you headed Don?"
She asked as we pulled onto the ramp.
"I'm going up to Cape Cod, June."
I announced as I was rubbing a cramp.
"Cape Cod, Don?"
She asked in all honesty,
"Where is that?
Is that in Tennessee?"

What could I say?
It felt kind of odd,
How could anybody,
Not know about Cape Cod?
"No, it's sort of far away, June,
Over on the coast.
About twenty hours from here,
Maybe twenty four at the most."

"Wow, Don!" She replied,
"That must be really far away,
Why are you going there?
Where are you gonna stay?"
"My aunt lives there," I explained,
"She's got a place by the sea.
We've been kind of close,
My uncle, Aunt Honey, and me."

"I know what you mean," She said,
"My Uncle Bill's like that too.
He takes real good care of me all the time.
It doesn't matter to him whatever I do.
Of course he's not really my uncle.
Just another friend of my Mom.
But I don't see him as much anymore,
Since she's hooked up with Tom."

"Sounds like your family is kind of scattered, June.
Oh, I'm sorry, I didn't mean to pry!"
"That's ok, Don. You're right.
Everything's falling apart and that's no lie."
With that she pulled her knees to her chest,
And curled up into a ball,
"Everything's a mess," she groaned.
"My life's all a big mess. All!"

Then she fell asleep curled up there for an hour,
As I drove down the interstate.
I figured she was pretty tired
And any more questions would just have to wait.
So I didn't disturb her,
She seemed so calm and serene.
I figured she needed time to catch up on sleep,
So who was I to intervene?

But when she woke up,
I realized I probably should have spoken.
"Where the hell are we?" she demanded,
And she surely wasn't jokin'.
She was mad as a hornet,
I had just knocked out of her nest,
"Where are you taking me Don?" she yelled,
She was obviously pretty distressed.

"No place, June," I said.
"We were just driving along and you fell asleep.
We were talking about your family,
But I thought it could probably keep.
You must have been pretty tired June,
You went out just like a light."
"Well, maybe I was tired," she said.
"I didn't get much sleep last night."

Chapter Four

"I'm sure you didn't," I said, I couldn't hold it back any more.
"But you could have made other choices.
You know, I didn't get much sleep myself,
Because I could hear everyone's voices.
And between all that commotion going on all night,
And the roof leaking rain water right on my face,
I had to go out and sleep in my car.
It was the only quiet dry place."

She changed her tune right then,
After I told her about all the noise,
"Yeah, I guess things got a bit crazy in there,
Between all the drinking and me and the boys."
We drove on for a mile or two after that,
And everything got kind of quiet.
"I've never done such a thing before," she finally said.
"Just this once I thought I'd try it."

"I should have known better," she continued on.
"Mixing my pills with their beer,
But life's sometimes kind of dull,
And it gets pretty boring around here."
I couldn't relate to what she was saying,
Especially about things always being so dull.
My life was always chaos and stress,
Or some other kind of a close call.

About that time the car started shaking,
And the front tire went flat,
I pulled off the road by the guard rail,
And that's just where we sat.
"Wow, that was a surprise!"
Said June, now clearly excited.
"I hope you have a spare," she offered.
Without even being invited.

"Yeah, my mechanic told me
That might happen someday.
Fortunately he put some air in it,
Seems like just yesterday."
The job of changing a flat tire wasn't a problem
Because I knew the drill,
I just didn't like getting so wet,
Cause it was raining still.

Of course June wasn't much help,
But I couldn't complain.
She wasn't trained for tire work,
Especially in the rain.
But she held a piece of cardboard over us
She had found in the back seat under some junk,
While I tried to loosen the lug nuts,
And get the tire out of the trunk.

The spare seemed a little soft
When I finally got it on the car.
I knew we'd have to stop for air
Before we went very far.
The steering wheel pulled a little to the right
As I got back up to speed.
That's when I noticed the cut on my hand,
That all of a sudden started to bleed.

I must have cut it on the jack,
Or maybe the tire stud.
June was frantic and let me know
She couldn't stand the sight of blood.
She started thrashing through her bag
For something to stop my leak,
Then she handed me a big pile of pink tissues,
Like I was some kind of a circus freak.

"Thank you," I said, trying to be gentlemanly,
Thinking maybe it would calm her down.
She nodded and continued searching in the bag
For something she hadn't found.
"My phone! I can't find my phone!
I'm sure I put it back in here."
"Look again," I said.
"That things big enough to hold a deer."

She darted a mean look toward me
And squinted like an angry dog.
I knew I was out of line just a bit,
I'd have to improve my dialogue.
June was throwing out all kinds of things from her bag,
Piling them all over the seat.
Lipstick, make up, hair clips, and more,
And saying things I won't repeat.

"It's not here!"
She finally announced in a near-hysterical despair.
I didn't say anything at first
Because it might sound like I didn't care.
"It must be at the motel!" she said a moment later.
"We'll have to go back there right away.
I'm sure my phone is there somewhere,
With my comb and my negligée."

I couldn't believe my ears.
This was crazy in the extreme.
Was I still sleeping in my car,
Still having another bad dream?
My mind was spinning too,
No, this was not a dream, this was a real mess!
And where things were going to go from here,
How could I even guess?

I tightened my grip on the wheel,
While my blood pressure started to rise.
"June," I said, "I have to get to Cape Cod,
Don't you realize?
I'm running late and by now
I should be just about getting there.
Instead I am still in Tennessee
Looking for a gas station that has air."

It wasn't what she wanted to hear.
She didn't care, I could tell.
"I have to have my phone Don!
We have to go back to the motel!"
And the way she said it I could tell she meant it,
Way down deep inside.
Before I had been talking to Dr. Jeckell,
But now he was Mrs. Hyde.

Those demure blue eyes darkened,
To the color of black coal in a pile,
Her face tightened, her lips raised up,
She had teeth like a crocodile.
She seemed to morph into an Amazon warrior
Right there before my eyes.
"You better turn this car around right now, Don!"
I could see there was no room for compromise.

It even sounded a bit like some kind of threat,
Anyway, I knew she was really serious.
I figured there would be no reasoning
With a woman this damn furious.
"Ok June," I said, resigned, but really mad.
"But we need air in that tire first,
Before we turn around and go back."
I was so mad, I thought my head would burst.

Chapter Five

"Good" was all she said
For all of the next eighteen miles.
But by the time we spotted the gas station sign,
She had returned to being all smiles.
"Pull into that one," she called out.
"It's a convenience store too and they'll have a ladies room."
As I put two quarters in the air machine I was thinking to myself,
"Ladies room, for whom?"

It even crossed my mind for a moment,
While the tire was filling with air,
Now would be a good time to get back in the car
And make my get away from there.
But I had to pee and I was hungry again as well,
So I let that idea slide.
I parked and locked the car
And made my way inside.

From there I proceeded to
The restroom for the men
Where, for the first time, I faced the hard facts
About this situation I'd put myself in.
Obviously June was a little different
Than other southern belles I had known.
She was a high maintenance gal and edgy too,
From everything she'd shown.

I'd been nearly two days on the road
And hadn't gone three hundred miles east.
Now we were going backwards,
And I'd lose another two hours, at least.
On the other hand, she was cute,
And honest and not at all fat,
But what was she doing with her life,
Running around like a stray alley cat?

I met her at the counter afterwards.
She was getting coffee and an egg on a roll with ham.
"Fancy meeting you here," she said.
"I thought you'd leave me, you know, scram.
I expected you'd dump me here high and dry,
By now I figured for sure you'd be gone.
Well, what is it Don? Is a new era starting for me,
Or is this just an exceptional phenomenon?"

I didn't know whether to smile or laugh,
But I sensed a different June.
Normal, fragile, and more thoughtful too,
And talking a different tune.
The ride back to the motel went a lot faster
Than going the other way.
We talked a lot about a whole bunch of things;
She had a lot to say.

Some of it was pretty crazy,
Like her home life and her mother's new man.
She hated this guy Tom like a snake
Because he had such a wandering hand.
She had left home about three years ago
After they all had a big fight.
Since then she had worked a bunch of low paying jobs,
And the men she met, well they only stayed a night.

Somewhere along the line at a bar
She had met a helpful shrink.
Her life was going nowhere by then,
And she was seriously starting to drink.
June and the psychologist,
They got along fine as soon as they met.
She felt better with his helpful advice,
And that occasional ride in his Corvette.

They met every day the following week,
And he prescribed some little white pills.
His guidance turned her in a new direction,
And stopped her from looking for thrills.
Pretty soon he prescribed bi-weekly office visits,
And for her they were always free.
Eventually she discovered he was married,
And apparently happily.

They also met two evenings every week,
For dinner and a few more pills.
But she ended it all after his love notes arrived
With the roses and the daffodils.
He said that was how he felt:
He loved her, wanted to build up her self-respect.
She said her self-respect would be fine,
He was the one who needed to show some respect.

His wife, she said, would never understand
Their little secret relationship,
So it was decided they had no choice
But to have just a little secret acquaintance-ship.
They parted on good terms it seems,
And he still sends her pills,
Which help her focus in times of stress,
Or get crazy in times of thrills.

I had bought a half a dozen bagels
And a giant cup of coffee too.
I drank it all and I ate them all but one,
Before our drive was through.
Pulling back into the motel lot
The place looked as bad as before.
June rushed toward her old room,
And pushed open the half-stuck door.

I was curious enough to follow along,
Just to be sure she was alright.
The room was bigger than mine,
But just as dingy even in the morning light.
June found her phone and negligee right away,
They were over by the bed.
She grabbed some stuff from the bathroom too,
Then out the door we sped.

Back on the highway my mind started to wonder
About last night, and why?
"So how come you spent the night with six men June?
I could understand one guy."
There it was, the elephant, out in the open,
The question every man would want to know.
It got real quiet for a moment or two,
Like when a bomb was whistling down on Tokyo.

Then she turned and faced me eye to eye,
Her blue eyes became redder than fire.
"You know Don," she said.
"I knew eventually you would just have to inquire.
You can't help it, I know, you're a guy,
A macho man head to toe.
"You'd love to spend a night with six women,
And be the only buck with the doe."

"What's the difference if I do six men in one night,
Just because I can?
For that I'm called a slut by everybody,
But if you did six women you'd be the man!
And don't tell me you wouldn't want to do that,
Every guy dreams of just such a day.
You're actually jealous of what I can do so easily.
You could never pull it off that way."

That wasn't the response I was expecting
From my pretty little blonde passenger.
I sat in silence for a minute thinking,
But I only got angrier.
She had a point though, I couldn't deny it,
I had never seen it that way.
Rights had changed but opinions hadn't,
They were the same as yesterday.

If women's rights and men's rights
Were really about the same,
Then each one could do as they wished
And there'd be no reason to blame.
But somewhere along the line,
Some men decided what all the women should do,
And having six men in your bed in one night
Was probably always taboo.

June could see my troubled mind
Looking at the thing from each side.
"Now you're getting it Don," she said.
"I can do anything I want, it's just not dignified.
But so what?
Opinions change and we have just once to go around.
I'd like to do a few things that I want now,
Before I'm dead and in the ground."

"Well," I said, "I guess the real world out there,
Hasn't yet caught on to your tune.
I've got to say though, you have a point,
But you're way ahead of the curve on that one June.
Maybe someday things will change,
And then you can do as you please,
But as things stand right now,
Everybody's gonna call you a slut or a sleaze."

"And while we're on the subject,
There's one more thing I'd like to know.
Who were those six guys last night,
And why did they suddenly go?"
"Oh," June said, "they're all friends of mine, Don,
I've dated each one since high school.
At least I thought they were my friends till now,"
Before they played me like a fool."

"They took off in the middle of the night Don,
Just left me there high and dry.
I didn't even know how I would get home
Until I saw you coming by.
I guess I was a fool to think I could act like that
And not be dumped and despised.
I thought that friends would understand,
But man was I surprised."

"Obviously they used you June,
And I can only hope you had a little fun,
But I'm not sure it was worth the price you'll pay
Before everything is done.
You know how people gossip and talk;
Your reputation is bound to sink.
Before you party like that anymore,
You ought to stop and think."

"I know. I know, Don.
I was crazy for doing what I did.
I guess I should have thought more about it,
I acted like a stupid kid."
"That's alright June," I said.
"You've got to move on, it's all in the past.
It's no use to feel sorry for yourself all the time,
Going around feeling downcast."

"Is there some place where I can drop you off," I asked,
"Some place close to home?"
"No, Don, that's the problem, there isn't anymore.
After last night, I'd be better off in Rome!"
"Well, June, I'm not going that far," I chuckled a bit.
"But I'd like to help you out if I can.
Don't you have a friend or a relative you could live with,
Somewhere amongst your clan?"

"You could stay there for a while,
'Til things calm down around here.
Then you could come back again,
Maybe in a few months or a year."
I looked at her but her face was a blank.
It was as if she didn't hear a word I'd said.
"Hello June." I called out in jest,
"We need to get a plan into *our* head."

"No, actually, I already have a plan,
But what about you?
You must live close by, I can drop you off at home."
There's nothing else I can do."
"Is your Aunt Honey nice?" she asked,
With a sly smile and a glance.
"Oh no June! Forget it," I said.
"Taking you to Aunt Honey's? Not a chance!"

"But I can't go back where I live,
Everyone there will know about last night.
My life will be a living hell every day,
Nothing will ever be right."
"Look June," I said, "You asked me for a ride,
You said, just a little way up the road,
And I've done all that and more."
By now I was ready to explode.

"I can't solve all your problems June.
I've got too many of my own,
We'd be a hundred miles further on by now,
If it hadn't been for your phone."
"Oh Don, I know," she cried, "You're right,
I'm so sorry, you've been so kind to me all day.
I just need some time to figure things out,
And find a place to stay."

I figured she had already stayed
At my place long enough,
But I couldn't figure out how to say it
Without it sounding too gruff.
She must have sensed what I was thinkin',
Cause she turned up her wailing plea.
"Please Don, don't drop me off!
I'd be like a refuge!"

"I can be helpful, I'll do anything you want.
"I can cook and clean and drive the car.
I'm not asking for charity Don,
I know you think it's bizarre,
But I can pay, I've got some money,
And a credit card I can still use.
I won't be any trouble. I'll do anything you ask.
After all you've done for me, how could I ever refuse?"

"I need your help a lot Babe," she went on,
"You're the only man who has ever given a hoot.
Just give me a chance, Honey, just a little one,
I'm practically destitute."
It was heart breaking, her begging to stay with me
Just a little longer in my beat up life-boat.
But those sweet words that she was saying to me,
They seemed like honey flowing right out of her throat.

Chapter Six

The longer she talked, the further she got,
And she could run on pretty good.
But that started to be OK;
Maybe things were starting to be understood.
We were certainly very different,
There couldn't be any doubt about that,
Whereas she was reckless and daring,
I was a planner, and careful as a cat.

So we went on a few more miles,
That's when I heard a funny noise under the hood.
The temperature gage was rising fast,
I knew it couldn't be good.
There was nowhere to stop but at the side of the road,
Right up against the shiny guard rail.
By then the car was steaming like a volcano,
And June was turning pale.

"What do you think it is Don?" she asked.
"Do you think it can be repaired?"
I didn't want to tell her I didn't think so,
Or that I might not be prepared.
As I pulled the hood release,
The windshield instantly clouded over with steam,
June grabbed my arm in a panic,
I covered her mouth to stop the scream.

"Don't be afraid," I said.
"It'll cool down in a little while,
Then I'll see what the problem is,
Meanwhile just sit back and try to smile."
I put the best face I could on this mess,
But all of my smiles were actually faked.
I knew there was a good chance that this time
The motor was totally baked.

Finally the car stopped convulsing,
And the steam died down to just smoke.
When I raised the hood it was easy to see,
It was the radiator hose that was broke.
Well, not really broken,
Just a crack that was likely to expand.
I fixed it with duct tape, at least temporarily,
But in the process I scalded my hand.

Now the radiator was nearly out of water
Because of that rotten hose leak.
Without water we couldn't go on,
But then I spotted from the road a creek.
It was way down the hill from the guard rail,
I could just barely see it through the trees.
My hand was on fire. "June," I asked, pointing,
"Would you get some of that water please?"

It surprised me a bit to see her so eager.
She climbed over the rail and started down the hill.
"Wait June, you need something to put the water in,
Something not likely to spill."
I looked by the roadside for a jar or a can,
And scrounged through the trunk all around,
But an empty quart bottle of vodka or gin,
Was the only container that I found.

June climbed back up and got it,
She didn't seem a tiny bit fazed.
I watched her go down to the creek bank,
Where half a dozen cattle grazed.
She knelt by the water and was filling the bottle,
When a big white van pulled up right behind us.
It was full of people all dressed up,
Everybody was in their Sunday fineness.

"We saw your hood was up Brother,
And figured you were in distress.
We're from the Calvary Free Forgiveness Church,
Here to offer our help and to bless.
What seems to be the problem?
Are you out of gas or did the old thing just die?
Oh, by the way, I'm Reverend Johnson,
You needn't be so shy."

"I've seen more problems than a hundred men,
Maybe a thousand, it's hard to tell
Most of 'em I saved, but unfortunately,
Some went on to Hell."
I could see June climbing up the hill from the creek,
But she couldn't see the van.
I tried to reassure the preacher that the car was OK,
Even though the hood was up, she still ran.

He was about to offer his blessing and goodbye,
When June called out in jest from below protesting,
"Hey Don, you can get the next bottle of vodka,
This hill is really steep, I'm resting."
Reverend Johnson's eye's got real wide,
His face got really red and as I watched it started to swell.
"Are you and that woman partaking,
Of the spirits of Satan in Hell?"

Before I could answer, he had decided that I was,
And he got talking about lost souls and sheep gone astray.
"Man, don't you realize you're a sinner?
You have no idea what you're throwing away?
If you would only call upon Jesus,
He would forgive you of every sin."
Then, as June stepped over the rail with the bottle,
I realized it wasn't vodka, it was gin.

She was surprised to see the preacher,
And probably half his congregation as well.
He was spewing out wrath about the wages of sin,
And the eternal hotness of Hell.
I told him I had a good idea of what it must be like,
Down there, burning forever in Hell,
Since my hand was still hurting from the radiator,
But he wasn't listening much, I could tell.

June just nodded hello,
Like she had seen it all a bunch of times before.
She walked right up to the sizzling radiator,
Took off the cap and started to pour.
Rev. Johnson, obviously a veteran church man,
Wasn't a man to miss anything unusual going down,
He stopped in mid verse and watched in silence.
That gurgling bottle was the only sound.

"That's as fine a use of those infernal spirits, Ma'am,
As I have ever seen in my entire life."
He said it loudly, as he embraced the congregation,
And a plump woman near him I took to be his wife.
"I can see your wife is clearly on a path,
For your salvation and it's well marked out.
And you, sir, mind what she shows you about life,
And change your ways and have no doubt."

With that remark everyone said "Praise the Lord,"
And then "Amen"
Then like a bunch of shiny robots,
Everybody filed into the van again.
I was standing there speechless, watching,
As the van pulled back onto the road,
Till June handed me the bottle and said,
"Your turn Don. Go get the next load."

I nodded as if I was in some kind of stupor,
After what had just transpired.
Then June said again, "Come on Don,"
"Get a couple more bottles now, I'm tired."
Well, it took another five bottles of gin,
That we had to carry up from that creek,
But it looked pretty good when I started her up.
The duct tape was holding and she didn't leak.

I was tired now and all sweaty too,
So I said let's stop and get ourselves a cold drink.
"Maybe there's a truck stop with showers too," she said.
"Cause I'm sort of starting to stink.
But we're not truckers June,
I don't think they'll let us in there."
"Don't be silly Don," she said.
"This is America. You can shower anywhere!"

Well sure as shootin', she was right.
After you paid a little money you could go right in.
Before that June decided she needed some clothes,
And started going through a discount bin.
She found a neon green tee that said "Peterbuilt"
In big white letters across the top,
With a picture of a tractor-trailer truck below it,
But still she wasn't ready to stop.

She needed cosmetics, a hair brush, a pair of shorts,
And some new underwear.
I noticed cowboy hats over in the corner.
I pointed at them and said, "I'll be over there."
After all the shopping and a shower,
We got double burgers, fries, and giant shakes.
Every time I think about how much we ate
My stomach always aches.

June looked great after a shower and in her new shirt,
And those white shorts that showed a lot of thigh.
I decided against the cowboy hat;
It looked real nice, but was too expensive to buy.
But I forgot I still had it on when I got into the car.
I studied the map to see just how far we had gone,
And it was even worse than I had suspected.
We were traveling about as fast as a mastodon.

Two days now had nearly gone by,
And there were hundreds of miles to go.
I knew June was the problem, that's for sure,
But how could I change the status-quo?
I didn't know where to take her,
At Aunt Honeys' they'd be like water and oil.
Auntie was old school where ladies acted proper.
I couldn't even imagine the turmoil.

I guess June noticed my stress,
Or maybe she could read my mind,
"Come on Don," she said, "fire this thing up.
We need to get back to the grind."
I didn't know how to put it to her,
We'd already been through all this before.
And it seemed like she had decided.
It was simply something she could just ignore.

She probably expected my thoughts by now,
Were about leaving her hanging at some dump,
But I didn't want to leave her just anywhere,
I wasn't such a hard-ass chump.
Cause she really wasn't a bad person,
And I wondered if I wasn't starting to care.
She cleaned up pretty good after that shower,
With the new clothes and clean, washed hair.

Still she was a little back woods looking,
But her attitude had seemed to improve.
Maybe it was just that she was shined up now,
And I felt like everyone would approve.
But I knew my Aunt pretty well from over the years,
And just clothes would never make things better.
Not even if she put on designer jeans and jewels.
June wouldn't pass even in a mink sweater.

Aunt Honey was also my god-mother,
Had been ever since I'd been alive.
She'd always taken the job very seriously too.
She'd do anything just to make sure I'd thrive.
She wanted me to succeed at everything I tried.
But I had fallen short so many times over the years,
And it troubled me when that happened
Cause she filled me full of guilt with her tears.

TOM SYKES

She was a lot like her twin sister, my Mom,
And I just didn't want to disappoint them again.
Somehow life is easier with strangers,
Than it ever is with kin.
If I brought June to Aunt Honey's
There'd be a chain reaction clear back to Mom.
There'd be chaos, shame, and blame everywhere.
It would be like dropping a nuclear bomb.

Then June spoke up, interrupting my thoughts,
"You're awfully quiet Don,
You haven't said a word in over ten miles.
Is the car ok? What's going on?"
"Oh, it's nothing," I said.
"Just daydreaming I guess."
It was hard to explain to her;
There were things I just couldn't express.

Chapter Seven

She looked so happy in the sunlight,
Just watching the world go by,
Then she leaned way over toward me,
And looked me straight in the eye.
"You know, you're my hero Don," she said.
"You've been so kind to me.
You saved me from that creepy motel.
I think you're the finest man in Tennessee."

With that she kissed me on the cheek,
And put her arms around my neck.
"Thank you so much for helping me Don,
My life's been such a wreck.
But you saved me, like my knight in shining armor.
And I was your damsel in distress.
I was stranded, exhausted, tired and sore,
Until you answered my SOS."

"You really are my savior Don.
I just wanted you to know.
You've given me a chance to find a new life.
There must be some place I can go.
I need your help just a little bit more,
I'll do whatever I can.
I'll share the load, I can even drive.
I just need a little time to plan."

"You can see I have to get away from here Don,
Start out again with a clean sheet.
I need a little breathing space,
Until I can get back upon my feet."
As she talked she moved a little closer to me,
And ran her fingers through my hair,
Then she tenderly kissed me again.
Attention like this was really pretty rare.

"I know you need to start over again," I said.
"But it's kinda hard to work this out.
I hadn't planned on a companion for this trip,
You know Aunt Honey's got religion, she's pretty devout.
It wouldn't sit with her too well,
If we both showed up at her door."
"Why not?" Asked June, quite naïve,
"Hasn't she seen you with a girl before?"

"That's not the issue,"
I tried to explain.
"Aunt Honey is pretty set in her ways.
She'd probably think I'd gone insane.
You see June, it just wouldn't look proper,
Showing up without an introduction,
She'd think we were having an affair,
There's no telling the repercussion."

"How could we be having an affair Don?
That's completely ridiculous!
You just picked me up this morning.
We haven't had any time to get promiscuous.
We don't even have any history, don't you see?
We barely just met!
We don't know anything about each other.
I don't have affairs with strangers, well, at least not yet."

"Surely your Aunt Honey could see for herself,
That we are just traveling around.
We're sight-seeing, taking a vacation tour,
It's not the way you make it sound.
We haven't done anything wrong,
Besides, the truth is on our side.
You're just jumping to conclusions Don,
We've done nothing we have to hide."

"Well, maybe not June," I said.
"But that's not how things will be seen.
I told you before, Aunt Honey's got religion,
She can be really mean."
"Oh Don, your Aunt Honey can't be that dumb.
You can just tell her we're simply on tour.
Stop jumping to those crazy conclusions,
You can't ever be that sure."

"Yes I can. Damn it, June!
I know my Aunt Honey pretty well.
She'll bust a gut when we show up.
She'll say I'm going straight to Hell!
I'll never hear the end of it.
I'd be like a fallen star.
A total disgrace to the family,
My reputation would be like tar."

"You must have some idea June,
Of just what that is like.
I think you would walk,
Or run or maybe even hitch-hike,
Just to get away from the mess you made.
If we showed up on Cape Cod—don't you see?
I wouldn't have any place to go to either.
But I'm considering the consequences before I have my spree."

I hadn't meant to throw out that final little barb,
I should have kept my big mouth shut.
Cause June burst out crying. Then she said,
"So, you really just think I'm a slut?
Not good enough for your sweet old Aunt Honey.
I've had enough of your precious image Don.
I hoped we could travel and have some fun.
Pull off at the next exit and you can go right on."

"But June," I countered,
"I didn't mean it that way."
Which probably wasn't true,
But what else could I say?
You just can't call a girl a slut right to her face.
"So you did some guys, June, that's not a crime,
Most girls have done that now and then,
It's just that usually it's only one at a time."

"See!" June erupted now, "You did it again!
I thought you understood.
I know I shouldn't have done what I did Don,
But I was a fool to think you understood.
I thought you had forgiven me.
But now I see that you never will.
I can't go on like this anymore Don.
Drop me off. I, I've had my fill."

"Oh June," I said, "Please, don't be so mad,
I didn't mean to hurt you with anything I said.
We all do stupid things every once in a while.
Actually dumb things just come into my head.
Really June, I do stupid things all the time.
So it's easy to sympathize with you,
Because we both have made mistakes.
I've probably made more than you."

"Please don't be so mad June," I said,
"We're a lot alike, don't you see?
It's easy for me to forgive you honey,
Cause nobody makes more mistakes than me.
I sympathize with your situation.
So let's drop this and be friendly like before.
What you do is your business anyway," I concluded.
"Business! That wasn't business. I'm not a whore!"

I was doing ok till I used the word business,
Now June was really boiling.
"There's a damn exit in three more frigging miles."
I pictured a large serpent coiling.
"You can pull off right there Don.
There's a truck stop there too.
I'll get a ride with one of them.
I really don't need you!"

With that she folded her arms across her chest,
And stared out at the road straight ahead.
Gone like a vaporous mist,
Were all the sweet things that she had just said.
How stupid of me to open my big mouth,
And say the first thing that came into my head.
I tried to say something that sounded better,
But everything I thought of was even worse than what I had
   already said.

After all these miles it had come to this:
Everything I said came out like a slur.
My companion was bailing out,
And I suddenly knew I'd be missing her.
I pulled off at the next exit,
Eased up to the intersection at the overpass.
"Stop here and let me out," she demanded.
"Let me out right here on the grass."

"I don't want to be a drag on you Don,
Or hold you up one minute more."
"Wait June, I'm not leaving you here in the street.
Let me take you over there to that store."
That "store" was a giant service center,
The biggest one I had ever seen.
As soon as I stopped the car at the curb,
I had hoped to intervene.

But June was out of her seat in a flash,
And quickly slammed the door.
I only had a second to yell,
That I didn't mean what I said before.
But she didn't even look back.
I shouted, "June, please, stop, wait!"
Then I yelled it again louder this time,
But my words came out too late.

Chapter Eight

It's hard to explain the feeling I had,
Sitting there all alone.
On one hand it was all that I had ever wanted,
To be by myself and on my own.
But, on the other hand it was all so sudden,
I'd grown used to having her around.
She was funny and cute and helpful most of the time,
She was actually the nicest girl I'd ever found.

I stopped at the pumps for gas,
Then put some more air in all of the tires.
The car was ready to get back on the road,
But I still hadn't filled my desires.
I had to find her right then and there.
I made up my mind what I would say.
I wanted to tell her just what I was feeling,
Because I didn't feel the same as I did yesterday.

I checked at the donut shop, it was empty.
And she wasn't at Subway either.
I looked down ten rows of trucker's stuff for sale,
Then stopped to take a breather.
I got a couple of glazed donuts,
And started to get myself more concerned,
Maybe she was already gone,
After all she was really burned.

So here comes those low down honky-tonk blues,
What would old Hank William's think?
And I'm just sitting here in a donut shop,
I didn't even have a drink.
Then I saw the lounge sign at the end of the room,
June might be there, but at least they'd have booze.
I headed through the dark curtains to look around.
I figured I didn't have too much to lose.

That's where all the truckers were,
Sittin' in the dark on stools along the bar.
I spotted June right away,
But things looked a little bizarre.
She was like the brightest star in heaven,
Like Venus or Vega in the darkest skies.
She was talking to these two big truckers,
And laughing, I could imagine all of their lies.

They were all joking and having a good old time,
While I watched from the curtain/door.
June was sitting right there in between them,
My burning jealousy was making me sore.
They were the biggest black guys in the room,
And June was talking to both of them at once.
I was about to turn away totally discouraged.
I felt like the world's biggest dunce.

She seemed so comfortable around lots of guys,
I had no chance of winning her back again.
Then one of the truckers, the big one on the right,
Put his arm around June and tried to pull her in.
She resisted as best she could,
But he nearly dragged her off her stool,
She wiggled and yelled, "No!" and then, "Stop!"
Suddenly the happy party didn't look so cool.

As I watched they were getting up to leave.
Each one had June by an arm.
It was clear that June was not willing to go,
And probably feared she might come to harm.
She was yelling and kicking them both at the same time,
But everyone there kept sipping on their beers.
They were headed out towards me by now,
But somehow I swallowed my fears.

I knew I had to be out of my mind,
To think I could rescue my lady in distress,
Cause I'm not a very big guy,
To get involved is this kind of mess.
But if I didn't stop them, who would?
So without any further doubt or reflection
I just knew what had to be done,
And I took a couple of steps right in their direction.

I blocked the path that lead to the door,
And I don't know who was more surprised
When they saw me standing there in the dim light.
Was it June or those two big guys?
But I didn't give them time to think much.
I said, "Hey, don't you guys realize?
June doesn't want to go with you!
Put her down right now and apologize."

My words didn't seem to have very much effect.
"Hey!" I yelled a second time.
"Put her down now and leave her alone!
Around here kidnapping is still a crime."
I don't think they could believe what they heard,
Or what they were seeing with their own two eyes,
Cause all of them stopped right in front of my nose,
Tiny June and those two big truck-driving guys.

"The lady said she didn't want to go with you," I said.
"Maybe you guys can't hear so good."
Now I was clearly in a serious confrontation,
And I don't think they misunderstood.
All three of them started yelling at me at once.
"Get out of the way asshole, step aside."
I couldn't figure out why June was yelling too,
Then I realized she hadn't yet swallowed her pride.

Which, fortunately, didn't take her very much longer to do,
After the big guy threw me up against the far wall.
June broke free from the other one then,
And screamed even louder when she saw me fall.
The manager came running into The Lagoon,
Just as the big guy had lifted me up by my shirt,
His arm was cocked back to finish me off,
When June jumped on his back to stop him before I really got
    hurt.

The rest of the crowd in the bar were yelling now,
And the bartender was swinging a bat.
The trucker noticed the resistance he was getting,
And tossed me aside like a hat.
Then he called me a few pretty crude names,
Then after that they made their break.
I was slumped against the far wall feeling foggy,
Slowly giving my head a shake.

The crowd went back to quietly drinking again,
But June was like Florence Nightingale,
Kneeling at my side like a heavenly angel.
I remember her saying I looked kind of pale.
She got a cool damp cloth from the bartender,
And held me up as she washed my face.
After a few minutes I wasn't stunned anymore,
I said, "Come on June, let's get out of this place."

She helped me to my feet,
And leaned me up against the wall.
She stayed right beside me there a minute
To make sure that I didn't fall.
"June," I said, "I'm so sorry for everything,
I never for a moment wanted to make you upset.
It just came out all wrong.
I need you June. I've liked you ever since we met."

"I want you to stay with me, June,
At least till we get to know each other some more.
You don't belong in here with those kind of guys.
You can be sure they will treat you like a whore.
All I ever wanted to do was help you out.
I only wanted to do what was right.
Please don't leave me here and walk away, June.
I couldn't stand it if you were out of sight."

"I can't believe I acted like such an ass.
I'm sorry I made you cry.
I never should have said what I did.
Please forgive me. Please don't say good-bye."
June had been staring at me,
All the time I was talking she had never said a word.
But her eyes were glistening now with teardrops,
As she drank in everything she heard.

She put her arms around me tightly,
And looked right into my soul.
Tears were streaming down her face by now,
It seemed she'd lost control.
"Oh Don!" was all she said with breathless lips,
Then she kissed me too.
My prayers were answered in less than a heartbeat.
It seemed she loved me true.

It felt so good I kissed her back.
I felt like we had crossed the great divide.
I wasn't thinking about Aunt Honey anymore,
I had June right there by my side.
It was good to see her happy again too,
And it felt so good to hold her tight.
Some kind of change was coming over my heart,
Now everything began to feel right.

June had totally captured my mind.
And I felt so different inside.
We held each other in the crowded store.
There was nothing I wanted to hide."
Finally we headed out to the car,
Walking happily, hand in hand.
I hadn't felt this way before.
All the world was a wonderland.

As we were leaving the parking lot,
We saw the two truckers from the bar.
I pointed them out to June,
And thought of running over them with my car.
They glared at me mean as mad dogs,
But they smiled at June like before,
Until she poked up her middle finger at them,
Cranked down the window and swore.

"Ass holes!" she yelled at them,
And made sure that they heard her too.
Then she turned to me and said,
In a voice sweeter than a honeydew,
"Oh Don, that was so wonderful,
What you did for me today.
You rescued me again.
Nobody ever stood up for me that way.

You are always coming to save me,
Every time I screw up and get in a mess.
I don't deserve all you've done for me, Don.
I've acted like I couldn't care less.
But you have always been such a gentleman.
You've saved me and I didn't even have to ask."
Then she laid my hand on her thigh and said,
"I'll bet you're up for any task."

Well, she was right, I was feeling pretty up.
With all the kissing and the hugging,
I felt like I could handle anything that came along,
Except maybe more fighting or a mugging.
I was sailing down that interstate in such a cloud,
For a while I wondered if the tires were really touching the
    ground.
June had rested her head on my shoulder.
Her quiet humming was the only sound.

I was no longer down in the dumps
Like I had been just a short while before.
June was gently rubbing my thighs,
And I could hardly stand it much more.
She knew how to make a man feel tall.
I was feeling like a king with a crown.
With attention like this,
How could I ever be down?

But the front tire wasn't getting that same attention,
And unlike me, it was going down.
I eased the car over to the side,
And listened for that flopping sound.
The steering wheel was pulling hard to the right,
And I knew that tire couldn't last long.
June was no longer stroking my thigh
Since she knew something was definitely wrong.

Chapter Nine

She was fully alert now, like the perfect co-pilot
Keeping a vigilant look out.
"Don!" she yelled, "There's an exit coming up."
I saw it too but I was beginning to doubt.
It might be too far away.
"It's two miles more Don, just two.
Do you think we can make it?
Oh look, there's a gas station there too."

But the front tire was getting flatter,
It had almost run out of air,
The timing couldn't have been worse either,
Cause that tire once was the spare.
Our romantic spell was completely broken,
When the car angled off the shoulder.
June was no longer a purring kitten,
And I was feeling a little older.

I slowed the car down some more,
In case the tire blew out or went flat.
The steering wheel pulled harder now to the right,
I was struggling like an acrobat.
I knew there was still some air in that tire
Because it hadn't started thumping yet.
We were both becoming nervous wrecks,
And my hands were starting to sweat.

June called out, "only one more mile Hon."
I nodded and put on the signal light.
"Do you think we can make it Don?" she asked.
"I don't know sweetheart," I said, "We might."
It seemed like forever going that last long mile.
I hoped the station would have some tires to sell,
Cause our tire was flat by now,
And I knew it was cooked by the smell.

We came up to a small country cross road,
I could see an old gas station down over the hill.
As we coasted through the stop sign,
The tire stopped thumping and everything got still.
It puzzled me for a second until I figured it out.
It seems that the flat tire had left the rim.
And with the wheel grating on the pavement,
Things started sounding grim.

We looked pretty lame pulling into the station too,
On three tires that had rubber tread,
And a steel wheel that didn't have any.
I could see the attendant shaking his head.
I eased the car carefully up the apron,
To where he sat by the office door.
We were safe at last, but what a letdown it was,
From where I had been a couple of miles before.

"Looks like you got a problem son," he said.
I hope you got some time to kill."
"What do you mean?" I blurted right out.
I probably sounded kind of shrill.
"I can't put no tire on that rim,
You done flattened out the wheel.
See, it's all bent over where the tire goes on.
Another tire, well, it ain't never goin'a seal."

"No problem," I countered.
"I've got another wheel right here in the trunk."
With that I opened up the lid,
And pushed aside some of the junk.
I pulled out the other flat tire,
And rolled it over his way.
"Here's the other one," I said.
"Now there shouldn't be much of a delay."

"Well, let me see," he said,
As he bent down close, I didn't know what for,
"It's a two oh five fifteen son,
They're not too common anymore.
All the tires are bigger now or smaller than that.
Used to be you could buy that size at any store."
"What do you mean now?" I was getting irritated.
"Well, sizes are different now and yours is a dinosaur."

"Your wheel size is right in between,
All the tire sizes that are popular now,
Wheels aren't the same size as they used to be.
Most of the tires are bigger for mileage somehow."
"So what you are saying is that we're out of luck,
Cause you haven't got a tire that's the right size?"
"Well, not exactly, I got tires and some are fifteen.
I just don't have the two oh five, you got to realize.

"Oh, that's better," I said.
For a minute I thought we were done.
"Let's see what you've got?"
"Well, I only got these two son."
He said that after he went into the back room.
"But this one's too big and that one's too small,
But they'll both fit on your rim."
I looked at the tires, it was a hard call,

They were drastically different in width,
And they both were obviously used.
"I don't know sir," I said.
"I think I'd like new tires, you know, not used."
"Well son, I don't have any new ones,
Used is all I have to sell.
I could get two new ones by the end of the week."
Customer service wasn't his motto, I could tell.

"I can't wait till the end of the week,
I have to get up to Cape Cod before then.
How much are these two odd ones?" I asked.
He didn't seem to understand the mess we were in.
I figured "so what" if the tires didn't match.
Besides, with another wheel I'd have a spare.
Finally June asked, "Well, what do we have to pay?"
June and I were getting impatient just standing there.

"They're fifty apiece," he said after some thought.
"But if you want both I'll sell them for ninety five."
Of course he had me and he knew it.
Paying fifty in total was like being skinned alive.
But what could I do, he had the only tires around?
"Ok," I said, "That includes installation, right?"
"Oh no, can't do that. That's twenty more.
But I've got an extra wheel out back. It's yours, alright?"

"Plus tax, of course, I got to pay Uncle Sam."
It was highway robbery and everybody knew.
But he had us and he wasn't cutting us any slack.
June and I were so mad, but what else could we do?
"Alright," I said, "I guess we ain't got much choice.
Go ahead. We'll be over there out of the sun."
I pointed toward the trees on the side of the station.
"Just give us a shout when you're done."

"Ok. But it's going to take a couple of hours.
My grandson won't be here till after school.
He usually gets here about four."
It wasn't two thirty yet. Did he think I was a fool?
"Why do we have to wait for your grandson?
We really have to go, and it's already late."
I thought he would get the hint and go to work,
But he didn't seem to care how long we had to wait.

"I used to do all that work back in the day, son,
But I hurt my back years ago and today it's kinda' sore.
Besides, I just can't take this heat either.
I feel like I'm right there at Death's door.
Never seen it so hot in this part of the world.
If you want, I got the tools out back,
The car lift, it don't work no more,
But you can use my old floor jack."

"If you all want to get right back on the road,
Wouldn't be hard for you to change them right away
I'd be happy to let you use them tools.
It just might save your day."
Then he started walking over to his chair.
"I'll be here with my beer to watch your progress."
He flopped down and put his feet up on his desk.
"But if you need me, I'll be right here, I guess."

Changing tires in the hot sun was a real workout,
June and I worked like a two mules pulling a plow.
The old man got a kick out of watching us sweat,
Especially when June put on her bikini, "Wow!"
She took my mind off the lug nuts that's for sure.
So we were done by mid-afternoon,
All of June's tender parts were looking good,
And I imagined seeing more of them soon.

It was a great relief to get back up to speed again,
And feel the breeze blowing through our hair.
I reached over and opened the glove box,
For my deodorant stick we could share.
It's part of always being prepared
For any trouble that comes my way.
You never know where it's going to come from next.
Or how long it's going to stay.

We grabbed some more burger and fry combos,
At the drive-thru place at the next exit.
The sun was low when we finished our meal,
The gas was down low too, I should have checked it.
But we were already going up the on ramp,
To settle into our monotonous drive.
The slipping clutch was a constant topic,
June was tired of going fifty five.

I was tired of going slow too,
But I didn't want another disaster.
I told her she looked really good in her little bikini,
That even Daisy Duke in her prime couldn't surpass'er.
She really ate up every compliment like that.
I could tell because her breathing grew deeper.
She told me she really loved to hear my kind words.
Now I was beginning to see June as a keeper.

But, every so often I'd explain again about the clutch,
And why we had to go so slow,
That's when June's cell phone rang.
It was her Mom and she was about to blow.
It didn't sound good right from the start,
Cause all June could say was, "I know!"
Of course all I could hear was her side at first,
But that was bad enough though.

Chapter Ten

It seemed like Mom was really concerned for her,
Like maybe she hadn't been much before.
"Don't worry about me Mom," June said, "I'm OK."
But she couldn't stem her mother's roar.
"Well, I knew it was bound to come out, Mom.
I just didn't think it'd happen so fast.
Oh no! Even Aunt Flo found out!
Yeah, I'm sure she was aghast."

"I know Mom.
I really screwed up this time.
Wait till I get my hands on Fred!
What a slime!
No Mom, No!
That's not true at all!
It was only six Mom,
And no, there wasn't a brawl."

"Well Mom, it wasn't eight.
Just six.
I know Mom, please don't be mad.
But it was really just six.
I'm sorry Mom." June said.
I noticed then she was crying.
"I'm sorry. No, it won't happen again.
No Mom. I'm not lying."

"Anyway, don't worry about me,
I won't be around for a while.
Yeah, I did. His name is Don.
No he isn't Mom, he's got style.
We're on our way to Cape Cod right now.
We're going up there to visit his aunt.
That's right, up north. I'll tell you more later.
But just right now I can't."

"Well I just met him,
His name is Don.
Yeah, he's from Tennessee too.
No. No. I'm not putting you on.
I'm sorry you don't believe me.
Everything is a mess, I know.
I'm sorry Mom. I really am.
But now I just have to go."

After a while June curled up into a ball,
Just like on the first day.
I couldn't make out the words,
But I'm sure Mom was having her say.
June was defensive about how things had gone,
Of course none of it had gone very well,
There was just no way of denying it,
Now her Mother was giving her hell.

Apparently she thought June was the cause of it all,
And she had given the whole family a big black eye.
June turned away toward the window then,
She was thinking I wouldn't see her cry.
But her Mom must have been yelling pretty loud,
Cause it wasn't hard for me to hear.
June said, "I know, Mom, I screwed up again."
Then she said, "No, it wasn't like last year!"

"Well, don't believe it. Mom, it's just not true.
I know it doesn't matter. I know I'm in a fix.
Well, yeah. They just left me high and dry.
Some friends, huh? No. No Mom. Just six.
But this guy Don, yeah, he's been a big help.
He rescued me from two big truckers at this bar.
No, I wasn't loaded Mom.
Yeah. That's right. Then he took me to his car."

It was getting dark by now,
So I turned the headlight on,
I should have changed that burned out bulb,
When we put the tires on.
But I was so hot and tired there,
I just wanted to get away.
June was trying to calm her mother down,
But she still had more to say.

I could tell June was getting tired of hearing it,
Cause she'd smile at me and then frown.
Mom wasn't ready to let her off the hook yet.
It wasn't so easy to calm her down.
Everyone she knew was talking Mom said.
The motel news had spread all around.
I guess Fred had said something at the barber shop,
And pretty soon June was the talk of the town.

June said something like, "let 'em talk."
Then said, "Mom, please. I gotta go.
I know Mom. I'm sorry that you're hurt.
But right now my battery's running low.
We'll have to talk about it later.
No! I won't forget to call.
Don't worry, Mom.
I'm really not a criminal!"

June started crying again,
As soon as she put the phone down.
"Mom knows about the night at the motel,
And so does everyone in town."
"It was bound to happen sometime June," I said.
"I guess the lid wasn't on very tight."
"Yeah, I just thought I might have more time,
So I could try somehow to make it right."

"Sounds like your Mom was pretty upset," I said,
Trying to offer a little sympathy.
"It must have been a shock, the news I mean.
Coming at her so suddenly.
Coming from you might've been better,
Than hearing it from the neighbors that way.
But it's no easy thing to bring up.
It's like an atom bomb either way."

June sniffled, then blew her nose,
And carefully wiped her eyes dry.
I knew that she was hurting,
So I gently laid my hand on her thigh.
"Yeah," she said, after a while,
"There's no good way to tell mom you're a slut.
And now's there's nothing I can do about it at all.
Except kill Fred for not keeping his big mouth shut."

"Don't feel so bad," I said.
"Everything is going to work out just fine."
I didn't know how that was going to happen,
But it sounded like a pretty good line.
"And besides," I said continuing.
"I don't think you're a slut anymore."
Of course I still thought she'd once been a slut,
But never once did I think she was a whore.

"I don't know what to do anymore," sighed June.
Clearly she was seeking direction.
"Well, I'm not sure either," I said.
"But some day it'll be beyond recollection."
I didn't have a clue what advice to give.
"You just have to keep on going June," I finally said.
"It's over, it's all in the past.
"If you can't look back, then just look ahead."

"That's easy for you to say Don.
How can you be so sure?"
"I don't know anything for sure June,
But you can never tell what's in store.
People die or they forget,
Or after a while they just no longer care.
So just move on with things,
Your life's your own affair."

Right after I said that,
We went by a cop beside the highway,
I watched him in my mirror.
He pulled out and was coming my way.
I hoped it was just a coincidence,
And not a case of deja-vu.
Of course I hadn't been speeding.
So why should he pursue?

But just to be on the safe side,
I pulled on to the exit lane,
Hoping that he was after someone else,
But all my efforts were in vain.
Next I pulled into a gas station,
Trying to ignore the flashing blue lights.
But then he touched off the siren just a bit.
I figured pretty soon he'd be reading me my rights.

Chapter Eleven

The place where I parked,
With him right behind me,
Was in front of a crowded little donut shop,
And everyone inside was trying to see.
I watched him get out of the cruiser.
He looked all business to me,
Like maybe ever since he was born,
A cop was all he ever wanted to be.

"License and registration sir," he said.
I mumbled, "Here we go again."
But soon he said it was 'all in order with my paper work, sir'.
He even had a grin.
Then he leaned in and asked me very seriously,
"Did you know you had a headlight out son?"
"Yes sir, I did," I said.
Then I handed him the other citation I had won.

"Things have been kind of tough lately," I offered.
"Don't I have ten days to get it repaired?
I haven't had a chance to fix it yet,
But I'll get to it real soon," I declared.
The trooper looked over the citation real close,
"Yes sir," he said, "You're right.
You do have ten days to get it repaired,
But till then you can't drive at night."

"You're kidding!" I said, hardly believing the words.
"I'm not going to get another ticket am I?
I didn't realize I could only drive during the day.
I'll go into this station and get a bulb that's new.
I can't afford another ticket sir," I whined.
But I'll get it fixed right now while I'm here."
He just shined his light in the car.
I figured he was checking for guns, or drugs or beer.

But he wasn't concerned about these things at all.
He mostly lit up June's Peterbuilt shirt.
I was glad she had covered her tiny bikini at least,
And covered her shorts with a skirt.
I guess we looked like regular poor folks to him,
Just down to our next to last dime.
He took a while thinking about the situation,
But the light was on June's chest the whole time.

"Ok," he said after a while.
"If you can get that light working again,
Then you can be on your way.
But I don't think Andy or Ben,
(They were the owners of the place.)
Have anything in the way of parts.
They mostly sell soda and donuts for the kids.
Some gas and oil but mostly bagels or pop-tarts."

"You may have to park it right here till dawn.
I can't let you back on the road with one light.
This place is a hangout for folks of all ages,
They're open every day and all night."
Inside it seemed like everybody knew the cop's name,
Several called out when they saw him, "Hi Bill."
I think he knew all of their names as well
Cause he lived close by, right over the hill.

"Hey Kevin,"
He called out to a young man over by the wall.
He stood up and looked from his corner booth.
He had the face of a possum, but he was tall.
His clothes were covered with dirt and grease,
And soon I found out why.
He came over to us scratching his head.
And looked at Bill kind of sly.

"What's up Bill?" he asked.
"Kevin, this is Don.
He needs a headlight for his car out there.
Or he'll be sitting here till dawn.
Have you got any cars like that one,
Sitting on that hill over by your farm?
Probably be worth your while to find one.
Least ways, it wouldn't do no harm."

Well, Kevin had a 90 acre farm nearby,
But he also had a junk yard there right next to it.
He said he was pretty sure
He had a headlamp there that would do it.
He seemed to know a lot about cars,
Both the old ones and the new.
But he didn't want to go there after dark,
He was hinting that he had better things to do.

June had been standing by my side listening,
But now she felt forced to jump right in.
And without so much as an introduction she said.
"Kevin, can't you see the mess we're in?
We'll be stuck here all night without your help."
Then she looked him right in the eye.
"It's not too dark outside for us, is it Kevin,
Couldn't you at least come out and try?"

"We really need to get back on the road."
Her voice was soft now like a bird cooing.
"I'll go with you and hold your light," she promised.
"Believe me, I know what I'm doing.
Please Kevin, you're the only guy who can help."
Kevin's resistance was melting fast.
Like a snow cone on the Fourth of July.
I wasn't surprised that he couldn't last.

"Yeah," he said, staring at her Peterbuilt shirt.
"I wasn't doing anything else tonight.
My truck is right outside," he said,
After that June hugged him tight.
"Oh, thank you Kevin," she gushed,
"I'm so glad we found a man like you."
I could feel my jealousy suddenly rising.
I was amazed at how quickly it grew.

Minutes later the three of us were in Kevin's old truck,
Slowly working our way up his hill.
There in the moonlight I could see all the cars,
It's amazing but I can remember them still.
There had to be hundreds of them,
Maybe a thousand or two.
Kevin was really proud of his collection,
Cause he slowed down just to let us take in the view.

He pointed out the different brands,
Each one had its own row.
Some of them were pretty smashed up,
But at least now you could know
If it had been a Ford or a Chevy,
Or some other make
Before it was piled up on I-40,
When someone made their last mistake.

Every car had a story,
And Kevin seemed to know them all.
Where they came from and when,
Whether it was summer or fall.
He knew all the models too,
And how they were related and such.
Which parts would fit other cars and what year—
I couldn't remember that much.

He showed us a complete 1950 Studebaker,
Resting on four flat tires,
But most of the cars had been in big wrecks,
And a few had been in fires.
Only a few had headlights or grilles not smashed.
Kevin drove along slowly as he re-lit his pipe,
Calmly eyeing his vast collection. Not just of cars,
But buses and trucks too, dozens of every type.

He puffed on his pipe a couple of times,
And I could tell he was smoking real weed.
He had us roll up all of the windows,
So we could all take in what we'd need.
The smoke totally filled up the cab,
I could hardly see into the night,
By the time we had gone up a few more rows,
I didn't care if we ever found our light.

But June was more focused,
Maybe her tolerance was higher.
Kevin stopped and he and June got out,
But I had no desire.
I just sat in the truck and watched,
As they wandered among the junk.
The light and the pipe and the smoke moved in the night
While I just stared ahead like a drunk.

At last they stopped at a car,
And carefully raised the hood.
They braced it open with on old tail pipe,
I guessed they had found something good.
June held the flash light,
While Kevin worked at something by the grille.
In a minute June was jumping for joy,
But I thought I was going to be ill.

"We found one," said June, moments later,
As she slid across the seat.
"And Kevin thinks it'll fit right in,
Wouldn't that be neat?"
"That's awesome dude!" I told Kevin,
As he got in and slammed the door.
My head was so full of fumes by then I announced.
"You saved our asses, man, for sure!"

My head was clearing a little bit,
By the time we got back to the store,
But I still felt lethargic and stupid from all the smoke,
And more tired than I ever was before.
I stood by idly watching Kevin
Install the bulb in about a minute.
I wanted to help a little,
But my mind just wasn't in it.

Kevin sure knew his car parts,
He made the job look easy.
But charging me fifty dollars to do it
Seemed a little bit sleazy.
But it worked,
And Bill the trooper said,
"You're free to go."
So we piled in the car and fled.

But first we thanked everybody
For helping us on our way.
That's when Kevin came over to my window
After Bill had gone away.
He wanted to sell us some good stuff,
Same as he grew up on his farm.
Said he never used pesticides,
Or anything that would cause harm.

It was his "cash crop,"
And he offered us a puff.
I was still coming back down,
I said I'd had enough.
But June was still interested after she took a hit
And asked how much.
I didn't want to go back up to the farm, it was late,
I told him about the bad clutch.

Kevin had a few joints on him,
In his pocket in a metal cigarette case,
Said he found it in an old wrecked Caddy,
When he towed it to its final resting place.
He sold June a few,
I think they were four for ten,
He said that was cheap,
Direct, "no middle men."

June was lighting one up,
By the time we got turned around.
She tilted the seat back,
And didn't make a sound.
I was just glad to be back on the road,
June was relaxing, just staring straight ahead.
In a big cloud of gray smoke,
That occasionally glowed red.

"What a nice guy,
That Kevin," she said.
"So handy and helpful,
A far cry from Fred."
Then she was quiet and thinking,
With only the joint glowing red.
Except for a word every once in a while,
Anyone would have thought she was dead.

After about half an hour,
She finally spoke,
"There's probably lots of good guys, Don.
But most of them are a joke.
You're a good guy and Kevin too,
And that cop for not giving you another ticket.
But most of the guys I've known,
They would have just said 'Frig it.'"

"They're like my mother's boyfriend, Jack.
What a parasite!
They promise the whole world to you every day,
Then they screw you every night.
I'm tired of the way things have been with men,
All their lying just to get whatever they need.
And then leaving when they've had enough.
"I'm sick of being a loser Don. I want to succeed."

I had to admit, I was hearing wisdom and truth,
And I told her so.
"You're right June," I said,
"I think you trust people a little too much though.
They take advantage of you,
Just to get what they want.
I think inside you are a really kind person June,
But if I may say, I need to be more blunt."

"You can't resist a soft touch, ever,
To be honest with you June," I said.
"I think you're a magnet to all the losers in the world.
You sell yourself short and then hop in their bed.
You deserve better than what you've had.
You can do better, I know.
You just have to see the good ones from the bad,
The real ones without all the show."

"With a little bit of training June,
Your life could be a lot better.
You wouldn't be wasting your time.
You wouldn't be a dead-letter."
"What are you talking about Don?" she asked.
"I know a loser when I see one!"
"No, I don't think you do June.
Unless he's a really ugly simpleton."

"I think most of the guys are long gone,
And way around the bend,
Before you see them for what they are.
Are you starting to see a trend?
By then you're just picking up the pieces,
Or, in this last case, just trying to get away."
"Well, maybe you have something there Don," she said.
"I've never known a man who would stay."

"For that matter, they never tell the truth either,
It would be nice if they never lied.
But they always do, it seems
I can't change them, I know, I tried.
It would be nice to look into the future Don,
And not know any more frustration.
Imagine finding the right guy," she said.
"Who would stay for awhile after ejaculation?"

"See what I mean June? See the pattern?"

"Yeah, I do. All men are liars."

"Only to you June," I said.

"It's like with tires."

"What? Guys are like tires?"

"Well, a little bit, but don't think new, think used,

You can look at a used tire and see things,

Like how they were treated or abused."

"OK, go on" she said.

"Well, you got to look at the guy, or a tire, up close,

Like inspect it closely before you buy.

"Some wear in the middle, that's easy to diagnose.

That means they've been too full of hot air.

Some wear on one side, they're out of alignment,

Or have gone around the curves too fast.

They're going to need refinement."

"And some tires are slick, all the tread is worn off.

You're not going to get any traction with them."

"Alright," she said, "I get it about tires,

What about the guys, what do I look at in them?

"That's the hard part June, that you have to learn.

It's tougher because guys aren't exactly like a tire.

They're a little bit more complicated.

They don't just rotate, they adapt and they conspire."

Chapter Twelve

"Of course women do too, but that's another story."

"Ok, Ok, Don, give me some specifics to look for."

"Well, there's so many, I hardly know where to start."

We'll start at the bottom, down at the floor.

See what he's wearing on his feet,

Are they sandals, or shoes or boots?

Are they new, beat up, polished or dirty?"

"Come on Don, so what? Who gives two hoots?"

"Shoes can tell a lot about a person June.

Say the guy you meet has a new pair of Nikes,

What does that say to you?"

"Ah, he's got money, he likes to maybe please."

"No, no, no. That's what he's trying to say.

What he's really saying is, 'I am looking for a lady tonight.'

See, he's really out cruising for a one night stand,

He's the guy that you want out of your sight!"

"But I like guys with nice new shoes."
"Don't you think they know that June?
They're setting you up.
Then they throw their harpoon."
"So I shouldn't think twice if a guy has nice shoes?"
"No, not necessarily, it's not a hard and fast rule.
It's an indicator, you put it with other indicators.
For the true reading you need more than one tool."

"You have to look at the bigger picture.
Let's move along, after the shoes,
Is he wearing socks? And what kind?
You gotta look for all the clues.
Or maybe he's not even wearing socks.
See, that would be another indicator.
Could be good, could be bad,
You have to find that certain delineator."

"That's when all the indicators you observe agree,
They all point toward the same estimation."
June said it all sounded pretty silly
And was a crazy way of evaluation.
I started to argue with her,
But decided it wasn't worth a fight,
Some people can only handle portions of wisdom.
It takes a while before they see the light.

Anyway I was getting tired,
And kind of sleepy as well.
I started to ask June if she would like to drive,
But she was tired too, I could tell.
It must have been near midnight.
I suggested that we should stop and sleep a while,
June agreed with me as soon as I said it,
And pointed to an exit coming up in a mile.

We came to a crossroads intersection after the exit,
It was just a little county road going nowhere.
But they had been working on it during the day,
And had a lighted yard for all the trucks there.
I pulled next to a big red dump truck and parked.
It was a good place to grab a few winks.
They also had a nice green port-a-potty there too,
The kind that always stinks.

We tilted the seats back,
And had just started to relax,
When June said she was cold in just her shorts.
I hadn't noticed, I was wearing slacks.
If I ran the heater we'd die in our sleep from the exhaust fumes,
"There's a blanket in the back," I said.
Now I could see the goose bumps on both of her thighs.
"Crawl in the back there and make a bed."

June thought that was a good idea,
To stretch out and sleep for a while.
It didn't take her long to get herself tucked in,
Even without the security lights I could have seen her smile.
Her head was resting on my green gym bag.
The rest of her was under cover.
It was just a passing thought of mine,
That at least tonight she didn't have a lover.

I couldn't get to sleep at all though,
So much was passing through my mind.
I closed my eyes to rest them at least,
But it was impossible to unwind.
Nothing was going according to plan,
And the plan was getting pretty thin,
I thought I knew where I was going,
But I only knew where I'd been.

And that didn't make much sense.
Aunt Honey probably expected me by now.
Tomorrow was her birthday,
And I had promised to come by somehow.
But things were a little behind schedule,
Obviously I'd be arriving late.
And things were getting more complex too,
Was it chance or was it fate?

As I was considering all of these conflicting issues,
June called out from the back seat.
Apparently she was having a bad dream.
"No! No! Not again!" she'd repeat.
I turned my head to see if I could help.
"No! No! I'm tired Fred.
Leave me alone."
Then she pulled the blanket over her head.

I had forgotten about the motel,
But apparently she had not.
Now it all came back to me,
And turned my insides hot.
It's those night-time fears you get sometimes,
In a strange place after midnight.
All the things that you accepted throughout the day,
Suddenly at night don't seem right.

And you wonder how things got to be like this.
It simply happens, one thing here, one thing there,
All just piling on.
Everyday there's a few more bricks to bear,
Then the path grows narrower with each step,
As it twists and turns and climbs,
Then the lightest loads become very heavy,
As certain things become very uncertain sometimes.

So much for my meandering speculations.
They kept me awake till way past three.
Finally, exhausted, I slept for a while,
For an hour or two I was free.
Till trucks and workmen started showing up,
To tar and pave the road,
We must have been a sight to see
As we made stumbled to their commode.

A few miles further on,
We ate at McDonald's and brushed our teeth.
When we came out I saw a wet spot under the car,
So I took a look there underneath.
It looked like the leaking gas tank,
Was dripping a little more than before.
A support strap had rusted through it seems.
It was something I just couldn't ignore.

Fortunately I had a ratchet strap handy,
I always kept one in the trunk.
I fastened the hook on a bolt by the drive shaft,
I felt stupid laying in the parking lot like a drunk.
But I hooked the other end to the frame,
And cranked it tight as hell.
June remarked how clever I was,
That I could fix everything so well.

We felt a little better after eating and washing up.
I put gas in the tank to make up for what we'd burned.
Then checked the water and added more oil,
That was starting to make me concerned.
June was a little edgy,
She thought some fleas had bitten her overnight.
I remembered what Joe had said before I left,
And I imagined she might be right.

But of course I didn't tell her,
No need to make her sore.
I was certain she hated fleas,
But ticks I knew she hated more.
She sat up and let the breeze blow in,
Cause the AC had quit two years ago.
The cool breeze brought the itching to a stop.
So it seemed like we were good to go.

We'd only gone a few miles up the road,
I'd just started to settle into the grind,
When June suddenly screamed so loud,
I thought she'd lost her mind.
She was thrashing around like a cat after a mouse.
"Don, it's a tick and it's on my leg right here!"
I was afraid this would happen,
I told her not to fear.

"My mother got spotted fever from a tick,
We have to get it out."
I agreed and we stopped at the very next exit,
At a drug store there about.
I went in and got some antiseptic cream, tweezers,
Some alcohol swabs and balls of cotton.
We didn't want any spotted fever,
Like her poor old mother had gotten.

I got the tick out and crushed it in the parking lot.
But June worried there might be more than one.
She said they never travel alone,
So we looked and son of a gun,
We found another one on her foot,
And a small one on her arm.
I rubbed on the alcohol and the cream,
But I couldn't stop June's growing alarm.

"We need to do a complete tick check.
There might be more where we can't see.
"They crawl around everywhere you know."
It all sounded like a good idea to me.
"But June," I said, "We're in a parking lot.
We shouldn't do a tick check right here.
There might be little kids around,
Or a cop might interfere."

"Yeah, I guess you're right.
Let's get somewhere that's isolated more."
We turned down a little country road,
And I got ready to explore.
After a few miles the road bordered on some woods.
"Pull in there Don. Go up that grassy trail."
We went along till branches started hitting the car.
By the time I stopped June was turning pale.

She jumped right out,
And was tossing her clothing into the air.
It was quiet and shady in the woods,
With a sweet pine scent everywhere.
"Don, damn it, get over here.
You have to do a tick check on my back."
She already had the Peterbilt over her head.
I nearly blew my stack.

I slowly scanned every square inch of her spine.
Even rubbed a few spots where I wasn't sure.
But she looked good, even better than I imagined,
So I ask if I should look for more.
With that she dropped everything else to her ankles.
It was quite a sight to see.
I did a deluxe tick check like an old country doctor,
Very slow and carefully.

But unfortunately no ticks were found,
Where I had hoped they might appear
I couldn't help but get excited a bit,
Everything was so very near.
June didn't seem even a little bit shy,
With everything hanging out for me to see.
She was more concerned with ticks and fever,
Than what she was doing to me.

Then just as quickly she was fully dressed again,
With color back in her other cheeks.
"Thanks Doc," she said, laughing.
"I haven't felt better in weeks."
"You're welcome," I mumbled,
Still in shock from what I'd seen.
"Anytime June," I said,
As if tick checks like this were routine.

"It's really pleasant here," I said.
"Nice and quiet and peaceful as well.
"Look, the pines needles are so soft like a bed,
Maybe we could sit a spell?"
But she had already gotten in the car,
Without acknowledging my obvious plea.
I was hot blooded, like in the song,
My temperature was a hundred and three.

116

"I know what you're thinking Don," she said.
As I inched slowly back down the lane.
"You're all turned on because of the tick check,
So I better explain.
It's one of my few personal rules,
I thought I'd explained it before,
But I don't have sex with guys I don't know.
That's the difference between a slut and a whore."

"Wow June, I think you know me pretty well," I said.
"It seems like you can always tell what I'm thinking.
You know we've been together for nearly three days.
And almost continuously too!" I said winking.
She giggled at my pathetic argument,
I already knew my case was shot.
"I'll keep that in mind, Don," she said.
"The next time you're feeling hot."

Chapter Thirteen

I think I was hotter than she knew.
This girl was really getting under my skin.
She was looking better with each mile down the road,
I didn't know how long I could bare it and grin.
My best friends were the ticks in the back seat.
So, after a few more miles down the interstate,
I asked June, "Roughly how long would it take,
Before you know me well enough to mate?"

"Well Don, I probably know you enough right now,
But you're too pushy and I'm not in the mood."
I get it," I said, "I'll stop being pushy.
I was doing fine, but then you got nude."
"Yes, but that was a medical emergency.
Unusual measures had to be taken."
I was glad to be of service June," I said,
"But the whole thing has left me shaken."

"Me too," she said.

"But not the same way.

I still feel like those bugs,

Are around here to stay.

And they're making me really uncomfortable.

Do you think they could be living in your car?"

"That's possible I guess, June," I admitted.

"I'm sure they aren't particular."

"It's creepy thinking they're nearby, Don.

We've got to get rid of them right away.

I'm scratching now before they even bite.

They've got to go, there has to be a way."

"One time, when I was just a kid," I said,

"We killed fleas at home. Dad set off a can of gas.

You know those aerosol cans you just let go?

Well, those fleas were gone in just a flash."

"That's a perfect idea Don.

Let's get some at the next exit."

"We'll have to find a hardware store June.

That will be the best place to get it."

But there wasn't a hardware store there.

We had to drive about ten miles to a little town.

It was in the middle of nowhere.

There was nothing else around.

I got to thinking about June
As we were driving there.
It might be nice if I took her out for dinner,
It would show her how much I care.
I cautiously mentioned it to her,
And she said that idea sounded great,
Then she thought a minute and said
"It'd be like our first real date."

I was still smiling after we got the bug bomb.
It turned out that instead of a little six ounce can,
They only had the giant whole house size.
We decided to use it anyway, at least that was the plan.
After we closed up the car, we would set it off,
And then go have our dinner,
There was a diner just across the town square;
Already I was starting to feel like a winner.

The hardware store was closing up
And the sun was getting low.
The town seemed kind of quiet.
Everything was moving slow.
"Let's set it off right here," I said.
"There's nobody else nearby.
Then we can stroll over to the diner,
Have a leisurely dinner and I'll buy."

I could tell June was warming up to this idea.
We walked hand in hand to Dick's Family Cafe,
Found a table right by the front window,
And watched the car fill with gas across the way.
I was getting a warm comfortable feeling,
Just the two of us sitting down to a hot meal.
When we finished all the bugs would be dead.
And our relationship might start to congeal.

June was feeling less stressed at last,
And we joked about what all we'd been through.
It was a good way for her to get to know me better,
And maybe I'd get to know her better too,
Of course I was thinking in the Biblical sense,
And so far things were going along pretty well,
But as we ordered I noticed people over by my car,
But it was dark and I couldn't see 'em very well.

It looked like a firetruck and firemen were there,
They were swarming like hornets around my car.
I wondered what could be on fire,
Then the chief arrived in his flashing car.
What they were doing there I couldn't have guessed.
Everyone in the place was looking across the way,
I guess not much ever happened in that little town,
But boy, it did on that day!

Apparently I had forgotten to roll up a back window tight,
And the mist coming out looked like smoke to a fireman's eye,
Suddenly this sleepy town had a car on fire,
And any minute it might blow sky-high.
At first they tried to open the locked doors,
But a locked door never stopped a real fireman.
They thought the bug mist was smoke,
And my abandoned car was on fire, man.

In seconds they had all the glass smashed out,
I just couldn't believe my eyes.
They were spraying in water and foam,
And none of them heard my cries.
I ran to the diner door,
Even though I knew it was too late.
Then across the square I ran yelling
"Hey, hey, stop! Wait!"

I was nearly speechless when I reached the car,
Out of breath and gasping for air.
"Looked what you've done, you idiots," I yelled.
"That's no fire in there!"
But nobody noticed me in the excitement,
Till I dove in the car and returned with the can.
It was still sputtering as I showed the chief.
"Is this what you wanted," I said, "Mr. Fireman?"

The chief put a stop to the mess they were making,
And the men gathered around, their hoses still dripping.
I think they sensed that something was wrong.
They looked like school boys heading for a whipping.
"This is all it was guys," I yelled.
As I held up the can real high.
"I was just trying to kill some fleas."
With that June arrived and let out a cry.

"Look at this mess! Everything's ruined!
Why did you do this? There was no fire."
"Well, ma'am we saw the smoke,"
The chief stammered and started to perspire.
"That wasn't smoke," she yelled.
"We were just trying to kill some ticks,
While we were quietly eating our dinner,
Over at that diner there, over at Dick's!"

"I'm sorry about all this,"
The chief started to say.
"Well so am I," said June right back.
"Look what you've done, you can't leave us this way."
Everyone's eyes turned back towards the car,
Where glass chips twinkled across the seats
They were wet and shining in all of the lights,
From the trucks, the street ,and a bar called Pete's.

Everyone looked back at the chief.

Nobody argued with June about the mess.

He took off his helmet and scratched his head real hard.

"We should start with a beer, I guess."

The firemen were listening and heard what he said,

And they all started to cheer.

"Not you idiots!" Yelled the chief, clearly pissed off,

"You guys start cleaning up around here."

Chapter Fourteen

We went into Pete's place.

It was dark and small, like a typical bar.

"Hey Chief," one customer called out laughing.

"The guys looked real good out there on that car."

"Yeah," said another guy down at the end.

"First time I ever saw your guys practice in town.

Makes us all feel pretty unsafe,

With those guys around."

"I'm leaving my car in my garage," said another.

"It ain't safe to drink and drive."

"Have a cold one Bill and don't mind those guys," Pete said.

"Nobody's hurt. Everybody'll survive."

"Thanks," said the chief as he grabbed the cold glass.

"You know I'm getting tired of things going wrong.

Remember last time at Jake's barn? There was no fire.

He was just making moonshine all along."

Pete nodded with genuine sympathy
As he recalled the sad details
About the fire beginning after they got there—
How they were all smoking and drinking Jake's cocktails.
"Yeah," said the Chief looking disgusted.
"But they were too drunk by then to put it out Pete!"
The mayor and the council have all had it.
And I'm getting tired of taking the heat."

June and I were listening real close
As this story was being told.
Meanwhile the car outside was still dripping,
And our dinner at the diner was cold.
If I didn't say something soon June would.
"Chief," I said, "We've got a problem here.
We're in a big mess, thanks to your guys.
And we need more help than just a beer!"

"He's right Bill," said Pete,
 From behind the bar.
"Him and his young lady here are in a fix,
Just look what your guys did to their car.
This is a pretty lousy way to treat guests
Who come to visit our little town.
Nobody will want to come here anymore
After word about this gets around."

I had to admit,
Pete had a good picture of our situation,
And it seemed like Bill was finally getting it too.
"Call Birdy over at his gas station.
I think he's got a Ford like that one,
Laying out back.
The motor's shot,
But the glass is intact."

"And give Bob a call at the hardware store,
Tell him we need a wet/dry vacuum right away.
And see if Bates has got a room at his motel.
These two are going to need a place to stay.
On my way back to the station
I'll stop by Wilson's U-Haul place for sheets,
Or, better yet, some packing blankets,
We can spread them out on the seats."

June and I were marveling
At how the Chief took charge so quick.
Pete kept handing him beers while he called;
I think that's what did the trick.
About that time a big man walked in.
I got the feeling right away
He was probably the undertaker,
All dressed in a black suit that way.

Any way he seemed a little out of place,
But he was friendly and everybody said "Hi."
Even though he wasn't wearing an old cap and jeans.
"Well, Bill, no matter how hard you try,
Your boys do more harm than good fighting fires.
We got 'em all that fancy new equipment,
But they still can't get anything right.
Bill, they're becoming an embarrassment."

Bill nodded like it had been discussed before.
They all knew it was true and agreed.
"First it was Jake's and now this mess downtown.
People are starting to worry, things are going to seed.
Confidence is down Bill, people are talking.
Things have got to be improved.
I'll do what I can with the council,
But some of them want you removed."

Bill started another beer after the man in black left.
I said, "Who was that guy, what's he got going?"
"Ah, that's Dillon, he runs this town.
Nothing happens here without him knowing.
Sunday he's the preacher,
But then he's also the mayor.
But the people all like him, I guess,
'Cause really, he's pretty fair."

"But what about separation of church and state?
How can the mayor be the minister too?"
The Chief laughed, "It's like two different jobs.
He's black on Sunday and evenings but during the week he wears
  blue.
The people here are religious. It's not a crime.
What he says is gospel no one can deny.
He knows the Good Book and the by-laws too,
He'll lay it all out there. No, Dillon ain't shy."

I felt a little better after talking to the chief,
And watching as his men were cleaning my car.
The guy down at the end sent us another round.
Everybody was so friendly it was almost bizarre.
Finally the guy came down to talk to us,
He said, "Hi, my name's Slim."
We shook hands,
And that's when June recognized him.

"Uncle Billy Bob!" she cried.
And gave him a great big hug.
I began to wonder to myself,
How many uncles does she have hiding under the rug?
Well, Billy pulled up a stool to chat
While the chief was talking to his men on his radio.
I was stuck in between them,
There wasn't anywhere else to go.

I guess Billy Bob was an old family friend
Who knew June's mom pretty well.
It seemed like she had a lot of boyfriends,
As far as I could tell.
Cause Billy was asking about a bunch of guys
That he said he and her mother both knew.
Said he used to like her mom quite a lot.
Now I was thinking he liked her daughter too.

"I see our fire department screwed up again," he said.
"But they're good at fixing what they break.
They've had a lot of practice," he laughed.
"They ought to be done around day-break.
Course that don't help you much now.
What are you going to do till then?"
I didn't know—I had too much beer in my brain.
"Ya'll can stay over at my place," he announced with a grin.

Soon we were rolling down a country road
In Billy Bob's old pickup truck.
June was in the middle talking about old times.
I was staring out the window like an odd duck.
Billy's house was a single-wide trailer
Resting on the side of a hill.
There was a path to it through the weeds.
Everything was dark and still.

"It ain't much," he admitted
As the headlights showed the broken screen door.
"But it's home sweet home for me,
And my dogs and furthermore,
And this is the best part, far as I'm concerned,
It's gonna all be mine, free and clear too.
I'll have her all paid off," he said.
"By the time I turn sixty two."

I didn't get much sleep when I finally did nod off
Cause Billy Bob's four coon dogs
Barked about half the night.
After they quit it was just the bull frogs
And they croaked on till dawn.
Billy's trailer was kind of narrow and small,
He had a little bedroom at one end for him.
We had a chair and a love seat and that's all.

Tuesday

June could barely fit in the love seat;
She had to curl up like a cat in a nest.
I leaned the kitchen chair against the wall.
And, like I said before, I didn't get much rest.
But Billy was a good host,
At least he did the best he could.
We had bacon and eggs for breakfast,
After I had chopped the wood.

He dropped us off at my car
On his way to work at the mill in the next town.
There were a couple of firemen there by the car,
Mostly they were just standing around.
I was pleased to see all the glass was repaired,
And the car was cleaned up really well.
The seats were covered over in U-Haul pads.
We got right in, thanked everybody, and waved "farewell."

Chapter Fifteen

It was good to get back on the road again,
Even though I was tired and foggy.
The morning sun was shining right in my eyes,
And squinting just made me more groggy.
I must have nodded off for a second or two,
But I woke up right away on the rumble strip.
Just as I saw a hub cap flying off from the vibration.
But instinctively I'd tightened my grip.

"You better pull over and let me drive awhile Don.
You're going to get us killed driving like that."
So we changed places,
And I fell asleep right where I sat.
Several hours went by while I snoozed.
I only woke up when I had to pee.
June had everything under control though.
By that time we were out of Tennessee.

Road trips are more fun, you know,
When you look back at them later on.
But they're a pain in the ass at the time.
You always feel like you're crossing the Rubicon.
And every decision is filled with fate.
Where making one choice cancels out all the rest,
It's like taking one road where two split away.
You never know which decision is best.

So it was with June and I,
Two travelers on the Interstate of life.
Traveling in that same capsule of time,
Through temptation, anger and strife.
"You're awful quiet Don. What's up?
You haven't made a sound."
"Oh nothing," I said.
"Nothing very profound."

"You must be getting hungry, Don.
I know I am for sure."
"Yeah. And I have to take a dump too," I said.
"How's the car's temperature?
Is it still running nice and cool?
It's not good, you know, if it gets too hot."
"Is that the 'H' is Don, where it says temp?
It was in the middle but now it's not."

No. The needle was on the wrong side of the "H,"
"You've got to get off at this exit, June!"
I had never seen the gauge go that high.
It was surely going to blow real soon.
Of course the traffic was clogged on the exit ramp.
After we parked a cloud formed over the hood.
But my bowels were cramping from the gastric strain,
So I ran to the restroom as fast as I could.

I was feeling a lot better a few minutes later
When I got out of the dirty men's room.
That is until I saw June and the mechanic.
Standing beside my car and a giant steam plume,
They were looking at something they didn't like.
It was there under the hood in the mist.
And as I got closer to the car,
I could hear it real good when it hissed.

"That hose," said the guy, starting right in.
"The one with the duct tape on it?
Has got to be replaced.
But the motor's got to cool down just a bit
Before I can do any more.
The best thing to do now is just let her sit."
Well, I'd been sitting for days and now in the men's room too.
Seemed like everywhere things were turning to shit.

We killed some time
By getting a bite to eat.
More burgers and fries,
And some tea that was way too sweet.
I was feeling bitchy and all out of sorts,
But June was like a ray of sunshine
Enchanted in the late afternoon
By that beautiful blue skyline.

She said she had never been to Virginia before.
"It's so different than where I come from."
I had been up and down these interstates;
I think my senses must have gone numb.
Besides, I was thinking about the broken car,
And all the wasted time I'd spent,
And wondering what was coming next,
If we got past this predicament.

The secret to being happy in this life, it seemed to me at the time,
Was to love issues, problems and predicaments,
Cause that's what life mostly was.
If you were lucky, maybe a few accomplishments.
But they were pretty rare, so it occurred to me,
I needed to change my thinking.
I had to let the up be down,
And the floating be sinking.

Otherwise life was going to be hell,
Which is close to what it was becoming.
I needed to become a lover of strife,
And a companion to constant suffering.
I couldn't see any other way.
Everything had to be turned around.
The good had to become the bad,
And then the good would abound.

What a simple concept.
I couldn't believe I hadn't discovered it before.
There'd be no more struggling,
Trying to work things out any more.
I could simply let nature take its course,
Come what may,
Let the worst happen,
It'd be better that way.

The worse things got,
The better I'd feel.
Cause trouble came to me
Like a magnet comes to steel.
I could see then it was just a matter of perception,
A little change of attitude.
Trouble came to me every day,
But now I was in the mood.

What a load off my mind this revelation was,
When I heard the new hose was seventy bucks plus labor,
And he couldn't put it on till tomorrow afternoon.
I fell over laughing trying to say, "Wow! That sucks."
June was a little puzzled I could tell,
By the change that had come over me,
But anyway she was glad that I was happy,
And I was just as happy as I could be.

That night we slept in the back seat together,
Under the security light and a U-Haul pad.
June was in the mood for some fun I could tell,
But I said feeling that good would just make me sad.
However June was persistent,
And convinced me it wouldn't be so bad.
Well, it wasn't.
Not every mindset is iron-clad.

There it was already,
An exception to my new rule.
Things that feel good should feel bad,
At least that's what they taught in Sunday school.
But here was something that broke both rules,
What was good was good.
And when I was supposed to feel sad,
Instead I felt really, really good.

This was a little troubling to me,
Cause I had just changed good to come up bad,
Same as at Sunday school.
But this time I wasn't at all sad,
After June and I had made love.
This exception was a very good place to start.
If there had to be any exceptions to my rule,
They may as well begin inside my heart.

Wednesday

The backseat was still a little damp
From all the firemen's foam.
But once we got used to it,
It was just about like home.
The street light went out in the morning
When the sunshine came pouring in.
We washed up in the restroom,
And both took some aspirin.

After the garage was opened up for a while,
I had some of their fresh coffee. June had tea
Along with some peanuts out of the machine.
This kind of existence was now paradise to me.
The more I ached the better I felt.
We walked across a field working out our kinks,
And up a hill to the thick woods behind the shop.
It was peaceful there; we could see the bobolinks.

Then we laid back on the pine needles.
The ground was so soft, almost like a bed.
We talked and talked for quite a long while,
It was like our hearts spoke the words we said.
Then after some more good loving,
We napped like babes till noon.
It was pretty obvious to me by then
I was falling hard for June.

She seemed so free spirited,
And she was open and honest too,
And I already mentioned her looks.
What else does a woman have to do?
She captured this man,
And put him under her spell.
I was hooked,
And we both knew it pretty well.

But that was OK,
Cause I knew she was feeling it too.
Whatever I said made her smile.
She told me, "An honest man was way overdue."
But everything that I told her,
Well, it really was true.
Before then I had felt old,
But now I felt all new.

After our nap we went to see George the mechanic
And got a bite to eat.
George had done a little work on the car,
But the job still wasn't complete.
He had been busy he said.
With customers, "Nearly overrun!"
We went back up the hill with our U-Haul blanket this time;
I didn't care if George ever got done.

Around five we checked in with him again.
The car was ready so I paid the bill.
We had some supper after that,
Then went back up to the top of the hill.
It was just getting dark,
The sky glowed with colors of pink and blue.
I never paid much attention to the sunsets and such,
Never had time before to sit and admire the view.

Evening was coming on by now,
But we were still warm without the sun,
Even though the air was beginning to cool,
We still felt hot from our fun.
Our hearts seemed to glow like fire too,
And I hoped they always would.
But you can't live forever on the top of a hill,
But what a life you'd have if you could!

The hills wouldn't be so wonderful I guess,
Or nearly half as fine,
If I hadn't first crept through the dark hollows,
Searching for a little sunshine.
That seems to be the way life works out,
But after this hill I never wanted a valley again.
But downers come along just about all the time.
Is it fate or free will, or just that thing we call sin?

We hadn't gone too far up the interstate
Before we both began to feel sleepy and tired.
I guess all the excitement had caught up with us,
After all, a lot of things had transpired.
We decided to stop at a rest area that was coming up soon,
Maybe stretch, pee and put some more deodorant on.
But after we did all those things, we only became sleepier,
So we snuggled together on the back seat and slept like babes till
    dawn.

Chapter Sixteen

Thursday

There's a thing about the start of a day sometimes,
It's that moment when you objectively view yourself.
All of your feelings, aches, hopes, opinions,
With an eye on the past, the present and yourself,
What you are, were, and hope to be.
Some days you may not want to keep going.
But with June's fragrant blonde hair in my face,
I was very happy with what I'd been doing.

We freshened up the best we could
At the rest stop's restrooms made of stone.
The water was cold and the blow dryer was broken,
And the place smelled like urinal cologne.
We had soda and chips for breakfast
And topped it off with half a candy bar each.
The oil and water were fine when I checked them,
But when I put on the brakes they would screech.

TOM SYKES

I know that things can't be perfect all of the time,
I had gotten used to that a long time ago.
But sometimes hardly anything is perfect,
And the best you can hope for is just so-so.
Of course most of the time that's OK,
But once in a while it's not.
Like having a car as broken down as mine,
It wears on you a lot.

Or maybe it was June now in my life,
That changed my way of thinking about cars.
Things weren't completely about me anymore,
Like the candy bar, it wasn't mine, it was ours.
I guess I had developed an aversion to risk
That I never ever had before,
Fixing a car that was falling apart all the time,
Was just another burden I bore.

Like some people who carry around an extra hundred pounds of
    fat
Cause they like to eat and fat comes with the deal.
My car offered uncertainty and adventure
Every time I got behind the wheel.
I liked not knowing what might happen next,
And I never really cared.
Life was never dull or routine that way,
And whatever went wrong I repaired.

This is what I do a lot,
I think a lot about what makes me tick.
I've become my own psychologist;
I talk to myself when I'm sick.
Or when I do something stupid,
And I feel a certain way,
Like I need to have a reason to explain it all to myself, and
  everyone else,
Just why I acted that way.

I've become really good at figuring myself out,
It's knowledge that has given me a lot of confidence.
I know that whatever happens to me or my car,
Well, fixing it will only increase my competence
When I deal with the next situation.
But I was tiring of this same old uncertainty.
The unusual happening all the time
Was beginning to feel a little like drudgery.

And unusual things happened constantly to me,
So every day was just about the same.
The days were becoming kind of boring.
The unusual had become a dull game.
I guess I was getting tired of it all
Since everything was all turned around.
The unusual had become so usual,
There wasn't much adventure to be found.

I was driving a car that was falling apart,
And it wasn't such an adventure anymore.
I was tired of fixing things all the time,
And never knowing I'd arrive for sure.
It never used to matter if I was late,
Or if I never showed up at all.
But now I had a destination in mind,
And a little girl with a southern drawl.

We passed a sign on the side of the road,
"Virginia is for Lovers," it said.
Then my mind drifted to others I'd known
As we both smiled at the words we read.
My others were girls from times past,
Faces and places of decadence and delight.
It was a collage of erotic moments I'd had,
They revolved on a stage with just one light.

I was thinking maybe June was thinking the same thing
Cause neither of us said a word for a while.
The sign made the wheels turn inside our heads,
While outside we still wore our stupid smiles.
I couldn't help wondering though,
If she had an erotic collage like mine.
Isn't it stupid, I thought,
The things conjured up by a sign?
Virginia was for lovers, damn it,

As far as I was concerned.
And we qualified as lovers,
From all that I had learned.
But we had never said the word love,
During all our romps on our primitive bed.
But I was beginning to wonder though,
Could actions speak loader than what we'd said?

I didn't want to be the first one to say it,
And probably neither did she,
So we drove on in silence for hours,
Until both of us had to pee.
Some people talk a lot when they're afraid to say what's on their
    mind,
Others say nothing at all.
I hoped that we were both alike in our hopes,
And each of us were just afraid of a fall.

We were making pretty good time in Virginia,
June loved all the beautiful scenery going by.
It was hot when we had lunch at McDonald's,
Where we had their big meal and pie.
We held hands at the table as we ate
And June talked about all the new places and sights.
"Wouldn't it be fun to see Jefferson's home.
Or go in a cavern and for a minute turn out the lights?"

I laughed at her childish fun about the cavern,
"What would you do in that dark minute down there?"
"What would you like me to do?" she smiled.
Of course what I was thinking didn't have a prayer,
Besides it was just a pornographic dream,
Some mindless sophomoric fantasy of mine.
I said I'd like her to kiss for the whole minute.
"I'd love that. But couldn't we maybe recline?"

"You're such a flirt," I said, and continued
"You know I love it though."
"I want to make you happy Don," she said.
"That makes me happy you know.
I'll do anything I can Don, whatever it takes,
To fill your life with fun.
You make me feel like a new person Don,
And the old June is all done."

"Don't change too much, Sweetheart.
I liked the old June quite a lot."
"I know your thoughts, you horny little stud.
I'm not going to join a convent, really I'm not."
"That's a relief! I couldn't make it without you June."
"Yeah, I know Don, me too,
I've been feeling exactly that same way.
I wouldn't be here if it hadn't been for you."

"Well, if we don't get going pretty soon," I said.
"We'll still be here tomorrow too."
So after a quick check of fluids in the car
We bid another McDonald's adieu.
We were getting closer to Cape Cod
With every mile down the road.
June could see me smiling in the sunset
Because inside me a fire glowed.

On one hand I was feeling so good
With June snuggled close by my side.
But on the other hand there was tension building,
And it was going to be pretty hard to hide.
We'd be at Aunt Honey's in a day or two,
And I didn't think we were quite prepared.
I didn't know exactly what I was going to say,
And June didn't know enough yet to be scared.

I imagined what Aunt Honey would say
When she opened up her door.
I could pass because I was in the blood line,
But she'd think June was a whore.
What would I say when the time finally came,
How would I introduce my new friend?
The Peterbuilt shirt just wasn't going to cut it.
On the Cape truck tees just weren't the trend.

Somehow I just couldn't mess this thing up.
June had to be accepted when we got there,
But I didn't want her to change her ways
Just because Aunt Honey would stare.
I had to get her into some nice new duds,
Something that told people she had style.
And some luggage instead of that old plastic bag,
Then maybe Aunt Honey would smile.

I figured it wouldn't be too hard
To talk June into some new clothes,
Especially if I was buying them,
And she could have whatever I chose.
It was going to be a bit expense I knew,
Building up a completely new look,
But she was pretty important to me,
And I was happy to spend what it took.

I wanted us to look like everyone else did,
Nothing that would give Aunt Honey pause.
We were going to fit right in with them,
Nobody'd be dropping their jaws.
Cause I knew from experience
That first impressions mean a lot.
So I wanted it all to go smoothly,
Otherwise everything would come to naught.

Aunt Honey was going to have to see June my way,
And not have one of her fits.
Just seeing my June in fancy clothes and a smile,
Would make her give more than two shits.
After all, don't all women recognize style,
They can't ignore a person dressed really swell.
If I could do that with June,
Everything might go pretty well.

There was no denying Aunt Honey's convictions,
She had a lot of opinions stocked up in her head,
And she would announce them freely to anyone
With just about everything that she said.
I didn't know yet how I would keep her quiet,
But I wasn't going to endure her condemnation.
June and I would be treated like honored guests,
Or there was going to be a confrontation.

If it came to that I could count on Uncle Ed.
He was the one who'd put Auntie in her place.
He didn't share her religious fervor.
He was a quiet guy, just wanted some space.
But occasionally he would put his foot down,
And Aunt Honey had to listen to her man.
Cause he was the husband and she had to submit,
And it didn't hurt that he was gargantuan.

But fortunately for her he was mild mannered,
Rarely did anything disturb his way.
But like all men, once in a while,
Ed would find he needed to get away.
"I need a change of pace," he'd say.
Then he'd usually take a long weekend,
Maybe go fishing up at the cabin
By himself or take a friend.

But most of my talks with Uncle Ed
Never had much to do with fishing or the lake.
He loved cars and had a dealership downtown.
He could talk cars until, my ears would ache.
He knew them all,
Every model, every make, every year,
And he could sell them like hot cakes
Cause he seemed so honest and sincere.

So if things became too tense when we arrived
Because Aunt Honey had blown her stack,
I was counting on Uncle Ed to intervene
And maybe cut us a little slack.
But if he couldn't calm Aunt Honey
And June was under attack,
Well, I'd decided about that already,
We were leaving and not coming back.

My visit was supposed to be a birthday surprise,
Something I had dreamed up a couple of weeks back
When I was laid off at the factory in Memphis
While they were fixing their old smoke stack.
Figured I'd take the time off to take a vacation tour.
I hadn't seen Aunt Honey for a year or two,
And since she had a very nice house on the beach,
It seemed like a good thing to do.

I figured I'd be welcomed like a favored god-son,
And she'd be happy I'd remember her birthday.
Though I couldn't remember the exact day it was on,
But just remembering would make it OK.
It would be a nice break from the Memphis heat,
Swimming in that salty blue sea,
Or chatting by the pool over dinner,
Just Aunt Honey, Uncle Ed and me.

But, like I said before,
Everything had changed since June came on board.
There'd be lots of complications
And situations that wouldn't be ignored.
Like: "What are you doing with this girl June?"
She'd be judging by the Good Book she had always lived by,
And really, that's her right, I accepted that,
But I didn't want to hear her prophesy.

Just being consenting adults
Didn't have very much pull
In Aunt Honey's religious mind.
"Consenting," well, that was just a lot of bull.
Everything had to be done by the Book,
There wasn't much room for flexibility.
The way she saw things in this world
Was black and white and not so mercifully.

She had called down hell-fire on folks.
I had heard it a few times in the past
When she would visit us in Memphis.
But I was hoping now those days were passed.
Because Aunt Honey had a good heart,
And she could be generous too,
When she wasn't thundering out chapter and verse.
She could be kind, even to her nephew.

I needed to find a way to prepare June
For the reception that laid up ahead.
She had fallen asleep right after lunch so soundly,
She could have passed for dead.
By now we were in Pennsylvania,
And the sun had dropped low in the sky.
I toyed with the notion of driving through the night,
Until a little voice inside asked me, "Why?"

I was as tired as June, I was sure,
And even more tired of sleeping on the back seat.
Passing motels with vacancy signs made me think
Sleeping in there with June would be sweet.
It would be the pause that refreshed us both.
When I thought about knocking on Auntie's door
I was more certain that we needed more rest.
There was no telling what was in store.

Chapter Seventeen

I mentioned my idea to June
As the sun was fading in the west.
"What do you say to spending the night at one of these hotels up
  ahead?
It would be nice to get some good rest."
"I don't know Don," she said.
"I never stayed in such a nice place.
I think they're too fancy for this country girl."
I tried to assure her that was not the case.

But soon I got it about the fancy hotels.
"I'm not dressed right for one of those places.
Everybody there will be wearing dresses and suits."
Wow, I had stumbled onto the perfect ace of aces.
Here was the way to get her dressed to the nines,
And be ready for the worst Auntie could bring.
"That's no problem sugar plum," I said.
"There's a mall over there that has everything."

In seconds I was on the exit ramp for the mall.
It was bigger than any I'd ever seen.
I figured we'd start at Sears and work our way through all the
    stores,
Nothing but the best for my queen.
As we parked and were walking in,
I carefully explained about first impressions.
June seemed overwhelmed by size of the crowds,
But to my idea about new clothes I got no objections.

At Sears we got some nice under-garments,
And a couple of pieces of luggage that looked super.
Then a couple of tops without pictures of trucks.
June took to shopping like a real trooper.
Next door there was a place that did nails.
June was shy but I told her they would look nice.
They had an opening right away,
But I was shocked a bit at the price.

Anyway, after that she had her hair done too,
At a flashy fashion salon.
I got a haircut,
And from there we moved on.
She was starting to change
Right before my eyes.
A prettier June was emerging,
And it wasn't just a disguise.

Then we stopped at a high end store,
I didn't even recognize the name.
But they had some sharp outfits on display in the window,
And when we came out June hardly looked the same.
They say clothes make the man,
And maybe that's true,
But they do the same thing for a woman,
I'm here to tell you.

At the shoe store June tried a bunch of them on
While I stashed what we'd bought in the trunk.
We settled on several different styles,
Casual, dress up, slippers, all nice, no junk.
After that we rested and had a bite to eat
Right there on the concourse.
June was excited about all her new clothes
But so much talking had made her hoarse.

After eating I suggested a new watch would be nice.
She smiled and nodded, by then she had no voice.
We found one for dress up and two for every day.
She resisted the necklace but I gave her no choice.
She needed some jewelry to complete her new look.
Just a simple chain of gold looks good everywhere.
Then a bathing suit cause we'd be at the beach,
I liked her little bikini, but there wasn't much there.

So we settled on a sexy one piece suit,
It was kind of a compromise.
But we both agreed it looked good,
And it was exactly the right size.
We stopped at a couple of stores that just sold jeans
And some casual wear.
We got a couple pair that weren't too tight
Since I didn't want everyone to stare.

They were closing the mall
By the time we got to the other end,
Which was ok cause we were exhausted.
Besides, I didn't have much more money to spend.
But June had one stop in mind before we quit.
How could I resist the direction she was pointing in?
She wanted sexy sleepwear at Victoria's Secret.
Well she did just that, and made my head spin.

The entire shopping trip went like clock-work
As far as I was concerned.
I had thought it might be an awkward subject
But there was a lot I hadn't learned.
June couldn't wait to get to the hotel now,
She wanted to show off all her new clothes.
She could hardly wait till I parked the car.
Nor could I! You know how it goes.

She changed into one of her new outfits in the parking lot at the
  Embassy Suite,
Then we checked into a room on the seventh floor.
June was smart to let me do the talking at the desk,
She told me she'd never stayed in a hotel before.
I couldn't believe she had led such a sheltered life.
Hearing her words made me proud yet humble,
It was like she was giving me her hotel virginity.
For a change I'd be the first and I didn't want to fumble.

The room was pretty large,
With two double beds and a giant TV.
June was marveling about how nice everything was,
And I really had to agree.
The view from the window that far up
Made her step back and took her breath away.
Said she'd never been that high and still sober.
"Oh Don," she said, "What a holiday!"

I had to admit I was having a ball too,
But I was hemorrhaging money from my card.
Sometimes it seems like money can buy happiness,
At least for now life wasn't so hard.
We called for a bite from room service downstairs,
And while we waited June modeled her clothes.
I haven't seen anyone as happy in my whole life.
She looked like that perfectly blossomed red rose.

Of course she saved the best for last,
That lace and satin secret that she had picked out.
She had slipped into the bathroom to put it on,
When room service arrived with a shout.
After that June came out wrapped in a white towel,
And behind her the shower was running.
"Let's wash up before we eat," she said.
I had never seen a girl so stunning.

Who needed food at a time like this?
I left it on the bed to get cold.
Then we got hot in the shower,
Then we got hotter a thousand-fold.
I never knew a girl like June before,
Her touch, her kiss, her sigh, her smile,
Her loving made me feel more like a man,
Than any other woman had by a mile.

I wanted to tell her I loved her,
Right there as the water sprayed out,
I felt I was holding a rare and precious gift,
One that I had never known about.
In that moment of heavenly bliss and excitement,
Time and reason derailed and then stopped.
Nothing else seemed more important to me
Than making love to June till I dropped.

And I think June felt about the same,
As we made love right there in the tub
Until we just couldn't move any more,
Not even a little rub-a-dub-dub.
I was hearing voices from above,
I was sure they were heaven sent.
They were telling me to tell her now,
But I became disobedient.

I wasn't sure she'd love me too,
I was a coward when it came to spilling my heart.
I needed to know she cared as much as I did.
I felt like a bad actor misspeaking his part.
Because how else could she show me her feelings,
Any more than she already did?
We dried each other off with the soft towels as I watched myself
    in the mirror;
I was a man in the glass, but inside I was just a kid.

We were starving and exhausted,
And fell asleep right after we ate.
But only for an hour or two,
We just needed a little time to recuperate
Before beginning our loving anew,
Which we did till way passed two.
Then we rested for an hour or so
Then proceeded again to overdo.

Friday

Of course we slept in pretty late
After all that we'd put ourselves through.
Room service brought us breakfast about ten,
And we talked about what we should do.
I was more tired in the morning
Than when we had arrived the night before,
I just couldn't imagine driving all day.
It just made sense to stay there some more.

It sounded like a crazy thought at first,
But it really made a lot of sense.
Embassy Suite was paradise compared to my car.
My only concern was expense.
But then I thought,
How can you put a price on what I felt?
Money couldn't buy what I was feeling,
So I played the hand I was dealt.

I didn't get any resistance from June,
So I put the 'do not disturb' sign right on the door.
We needed to rest up for the final leg of the trip.
But first I needed to love her some more.
You know, it's hard to make love that many times,
And not say "I love you" to your partner.
But somehow we did it,
Like she was the lady and I the gardener.

I wondered how long this could go on,
Making love and never naming it.
Doing all the essential things one does,
And then never claiming it.
I couldn't help but feel
That she should have said something by now.
After all she had said nearly everything else,
Everything else but that vow.

Was she was burning for me
Like I was burning for her
So much that we couldn't let go of each other
While the hours went by in a blur?
She must be feeling what I was feeling, I concluded.
She must be just waiting for me
To be the first to say the words
And make that solemn decree.

It was driving me crazy as hell.
I just had to know for sure,
Was she feeling the same about me,
Or was all her loving for me just a lure?
The very thought made me shiver,
That her heart would be that cold.
Was she only a lonely little nympho,
Who never wanted to get old?

I realized I didn't need to be driving in my car
To still be taking a trip.
Things are happening all the time in your mind,
Whether you're alone or have companionship.
With June, even though we were doing a lot of the same things
    over and over,
I was slowly learning more about her each day,
Like the things she liked or worried about,
And the things that she liked me to say.

I didn't like all that I learned,
But I was glad she had shared what she knew,
Cause you can't just go up and down all the time,
In between you need some more personal glue.
The kind that bonds the physical with the internal
And lets you know where you stand.
It lets you see whether you want to know more
Or maybe just want to disband.

Well, I didn't want to disband.
I was becoming sort of addicted to June,
But everything was moving so quickly.
And we'd be at Aunt Honey's soon.
Another day at the Embassy
Seemed like the perfect recipe,
For resting, planning, and preparing,
And expanding our felicity.

I wasn't sure how much further it could expand
Before it would simply explode.
I was living in a fantastic wonderland,
A Garden of Eden on the side of the road.
Here all my needs were all being met
With only a touch or a kindly word.
It was a reality that I knew wasn't real,
A celestial alignment must have occurred.

Such a paradise could not be sustained forever,
At least not on my salary.
Serious plans were going to have to be made
To continue our luxury.
But even if it was just a fraction of the heaven
That I had lately been shown,
It would be paradise enough for me,
And a lot more than I'd ever known.

I wanted to invest in a pleasure annuity,
But I didn't know who I should see.
When I looked in the mirror on the closet door,
I only saw naked June and me.
That's when I realized
I had already made my investment,
And I was enjoying the dividends right now.
I knew it was money well spent.

Saturday

After breakfast while June was taking a shower,
I looked up Aunt Honey's number to give her a call.
I could give her a little heads up at least,
On what was about to fall.
I didn't want to use June's personal cell,
Besides, the Embassy had a phone.
I suspected Aunt Honey knew I was coming by now,
And I didn't want her to worry since I hadn't yet shown.

I dialed the number with trembling hands,
Not sure yet what I was going to say.
It rang a few times on the other end,
Then I heard Aunt Honey's message play.
"Hi Aunt Honey, it's Don," I said.
Then I couldn't think of anything else to say.
"I'm on my way to your house Aunt Honey.
I should be there tomorrow or the next day."

Chapter Eighteen

"I'll try again later," I said.
"I might catch you when you're in."
And then I hung up feeling stupid,
Or maybe it was the guilt of sin.
But why should she bother me so much?
I really needed to get a new life.
Then it hit me like a bowling ball.
Life rhymed with wife.

That's when June stepped out of the bathroom,
She was gorgeous even though she was dressed.
Those tight jeans and the pretty pink blouse,
Made her prettier than I could have guessed.
"Wow, June!" I said in a burst of excitement.
"I love you in that new outfit!"
At last I have used the word love,
But it was the only word that fit.

June was so happy,
She spun around for a three sixty view.
Her blonde hair sprayed out into the air,
And right then I just knew.
Something moved in the universe.
I felt it right in my soul.
It was love with a capital L,
And I didn't care if I lost control.

It didn't matter anymore
What her reaction would be.
I had to express my love right then,
Because it was consuming me.
You can call it sorcery,
Or you could call it fate,
Call it lunacy if you like,
But I had found my mate.

"June," I said as I reached for her hand.
"Please come here a minute and sit by me.
I've been thinking about something for a while."
She sat on the bed and put her hand on my knee.
"Why so serious all of the sudden?"
I think my tone made her smile go away.
"I am serious June, I've worried about this for a while."
"You worry me Don, what are you trying to say?"

"This is it June, but I don't know how you'll take it.
We've only been together a matter of days."
As I spoke her smiling face disappeared in a frown.
"Don't tell me Don, we're going our separate ways!
It always ends like this, Don.
Just when I think I've found the one.
But I'm used to it by now buddy.
So go on and have your fun."

"No June, you're not getting the picture at all.
I'm not going to leave you now or ever,
I'm yours for as long as you'll have me.
There's no one else but you forever."
Her blue eyes were wet with tears,
She was shocked and in confusion.
"June," I said, "I love you.
And Sweetheart, it's no illusion."

I had hoped when I finished,
That she would tenderly hug me,
And say the same words of love.
You know, repeat them back to me.
Punctuated perhaps with a her passionate kisses,
Like so many times before.
But she only sobbed with her head hanging down,
Staring straight at the floor.

I was puzzled to say the least,
Was this rejection or was it a mutual feeling?
In that minute I had no way to know.
"Oh Don!" she finally cried out, kneeling,
With mascara running down both of her cheeks.
"I know what you're feeling inside.
But I've heard it all before Babe.
And every time they've lied."

"I have heard 'I love you' so much,
It's become just another hook in my heart,
But it never gets reeled in.
So many times things looked good at the start,
Like everything begins with a bang,
But in time things come out from my past
That aren't so very good,
And my lovers go Don. They never last."

"This one will June!" I pleaded.
"I know you have had some bad breaks,
But I love you just the way you are right now.
The past is over, we've all made mistakes."
"Don, you hardly know a thing about me," she said.
"We've only been together a week.
How can you love what you don't even know?
My life is a pretty black streak."

"There's nothing you can say that will change my mind.
Don't reject me because of the others you knew.
Give me a chance to prove my love.
Haven't I been your friend and your lover too?
Well, I need your love and friendship too June.
True, we have not known each other for long,
But it's the greatest week I have ever known!
Please don't say what I feel is wrong."

"It's not wrong Honey,
It's not wrong at all,
But it scares me to hear you say it to me.
Every time I hear it I fall."
"It won't happen this time June," I pleaded.
"I don't want anything in return.
Just say you want to stay by my side.
I love you so much I burn."

"I'm not going anywhere Don,
You know I've got no place to go.
So cool your jets, I'm right here with you.
Besides if I go, I'll be sure to let you know."
Well, that wasn't as bad as I had feared at first,
But it wasn't the answer I really wanted to hear.
But at least now we could continue on,
And my deep feelings for her were clear.

I felt a release of energy in that moment.
It was good to tell her what I felt inside.
I needed to know just where we stood,
Because my heart was my only guide.
June seemed less tense too,
Now that we had expressed ourselves so clearly.
She went back into the bathroom and undressed,
Then we made love again, now more sincerely.

It's hard to rest when you're in heat all the time,
Even in an air conditioned room.
Two days at the Embassy nearly wore me out,
But my love continued to bloom.
In between eating, sleeping and loving,
I got to talk to Aunt Honey on the phone.
I told her I was bringing my girlfriend with me,
And I was surprised when she didn't groan.

She didn't even seem to notice what I'd said.
She sounded different, like a lion that was tame.
She wasn't her old bubbly self this time,
She sounded down, like not in the game.
But she was glad to hear that I was coming,
Though not in her old exuberant way.
Finally she said she'd roll out the welcome mat,
And asked how long we'd stay.

I was relieved to have broken the ice with Auntie,
About my coming up to her house with June.
But I was puzzled that she didn't make a fuss.
I guess I had expected a roaring dragoon.
Now that I had expressed my love to June,
And told Auntie I was bringing her to the Cape,
I was more relaxed than at any time on our trip.
Letting go of your feelings is really a great escape.

Sunday

We were still tired the next morning,
So we decided to sleep in a bit.
Eventually we got the shopping bags packed up,
But some of the plastic ones had started to split.
It had been raining most of the night,
And looked like it would continue all day.
If only I had a little more credit left on my card,
I would have said, "Let's just stay."

I went to bring the car up to the door—
I thought I'd look pretty smart.
But after running in the rain to the car,
The son of a bitch wouldn't start.
The battery had died after sitting idle for two days,
And I was so mad I began to twitch.
Turning the key only made a little click,
There was nothing I could do but bitch.

June comforted me when I got back to the room;
She showed me things we could do while it poured.
That took my mind off the car for a while,
In fact my whole attitude was restored.
We stayed in the room till the rain let up a bit,
Then we loaded the car with our stuff.
We pushed it across the lot while I popped the clutch.
We were lucky, one push was enough.

She started right up so we headed out.
Everything seemed to be going pretty good.
I was getting back up to our speed on the interstate,
When a gust of wind tore off the hood.
Apparently in the rain and rush in the parking lot,
The hood didn't get properly latched.
Well, the wind flipped it back onto the roof,
But the hinges still stayed attached.

Of course it all happened kind of quickly,
And fortunately I wasn't hurt too bad,
But I couldn't see a thing out the windshield at all,
And the whole episode was making me mad.
I got my window rolled down,
And hung my head outside,
As I eased over the rumble strip and stopped.
June was stunned and wide-eyed

She was a little frantic at first,
But it was business as usual for me.
I pushed the roof back up with my feet,
And folded the hood down so I could see.
Then with an old hammer from the trunk,
And a ratchet strap and some twine,
I lashed the hood to the fenders and the grille,
And in minutes we were back on the line.

I think June was really impressed
That I could handle such an emergency unfazed.
But then it comes with my attitude
Of expecting lots of trouble always.
Besides, I was concerned that the police would see I had a
    problem,
And make a fuss that would slow us down.
I didn't want any tow trucks to pay either,
Or any more do-gooders hanging around.

Later in the morning, about eleven,
I fell completely asleep at the wheel.
Fortunately June noticed in time,
And right after that we made a deal.
She would drive for a while,
And I could sleep some more.
But she was still a little uneasy
That the hood would fly off like before.

I cautioned her to watch the water temperature,
The oil pressure, and the gas gauge.
Then I curled up in the U Haul blanket,
And went to sleep like I imagined old age.
When I woke up we were in New Jersey.
June announced it as we crossed over the line.
I think she was tired of driving any further,
And by now I was rested just fine.

"No wonder people move south," she said.
"I never saw so much traffic before.
There were some big wrecks back there Don."
I said to myself, "there'll be more."
June had parked at a big service center,
So we went inside to eat.
It was the usual road food with coffee or soda,
But with June there it seemed like a treat.

Our conversations were easier now too,
More flippant and relaxed than they had been.
We shared our fries and pizza and drinks.
Her innocent wonder made me grin.
"How much farther do we have to go now Don,
We've been driving for how many days?"
"Well, we're way over half way now," I said.
"I'd say by now we're in the final phase."

Before we left I got gas and added oil.
It took me a while to untie the hood.
But the new radiator hose was holding up fine,
And everything else there looked good.
Some people stared as I fastened the hood down.
They were driving fancy cars and trucks,
Unlike mine they were shiny and new,
And must have cost big bucks.

But there is freedom having a beat up old car,
Cause you never worry about scratches or a dent.
No need to wash or wax or fuss much at all,
You can just drive it and be content.
But I had to admit, my car looked like hell
Compared to all the new ones flashing past.
I started to think I'd prefer something better,
After all, how much longer could this one last?

Anyway I had plenty of other things to think about
As we got closer to New York City.
The traffic was terrible with trucks everywhere,
And the litter and junk looked shitty.
Lots of garbage scattered on the sides of the road.
It didn't bother me much, I'd seen it all before,
But June was troubled by the whole mess.
It was a thing she just couldn't ignore.

"How can people live like this?" she asked.
"They're packed in here like rats in a cage.
No wonder they go berserk,
And start shooting up people in a rage."
"Oh, that doesn't happen as much as you think.
They live here because they think it's the best.
Everybody thinks that way. It's their home town,
It's always better than all of the rest."

"Maybe, but I think they're crazy,
I wouldn't live here on a bet.
I know, but they wouldn't live in Tennessee.
Here, all their needs are met."
The traffic at the G W Bridge was stopped.
It was hour or so before it started to crawl.
But it gave us plenty of time to see the city;
June had never seen so many buildings that tall.

It was dark by the time we got across the Hudson,
But the Cross Bronx wasn't moving much faster.
June was so frustrated with all the dirt and delays,
She thought it was all a disaster.
It was late by the time we got into Connecticut,
And we were worn out from driving all day.
"Don," June sighed, "Let's find another Embassy Suite.
Isn't your aunt still pretty far away?

I know it's expensive," she said.
"But this time I'll put it on my card.
We could take a hot bath together," she winked.
Of course saying "yes!" wasn't hard.
Now the place we got was really expensive,
And even fancier than the one before.
Being together in such a nice place
Made us both giggle as we unlocked the door.

Of course we weren't too tired for more loving
Before we settled down into dreamland.
June and I were becoming a pair it seemed.
Things were coming together as if they were planned.
The next morning we had the continental breakfast,
And June was looking down right elegant.
She seemed to be adapting to fancy hotels very well,
If only they weren't so extravagant.

Monday

June also liked the scenery better than New Jersey,
Especially when we drove near the Sound.
But of course we saw some crummy areas too,
Cause every place you go has some poverty around.
But most of the time the view was quite pleasant,
And it helped that the skies were now clear.
The sun had come out and dried up the road,
So I could just sit back and steer.

About noon we decided to stop.
We needed more gas and food.
But when I pushed the brake pedal down,
It didn't work the way that it should.
The pedal went right to the floor,
And our momentum never slowed.
Every time that happens it surprises me,
Even on the open road.

But I pumped the pedal a few times,
And the car slowed down like it should, at first,
But soon the pedal went down to the floor again.
I was thinking maybe a brake line had burst,
But when I pumped it some more,
The brakes worked again, but just not as well.
I got the car stopped finally with the parking brake,
But it was smoking and started to smell.

I burned up the parking brake
In my eagerness trying to survive.
June was looking white as a ghost,
But felt lucky to be alive.
I untied the bindings that held down the hood,
And carefully raised it until it began to kink.
The brake fluid reservoir was out of fluid.
I think by now we all needed a drink.

Apparently the fluid had leaked out,
Just the way Joe had said it would.
I would have checked it more often
If it was easier to open the hood.
I emptied a bottle of brake fluid from the trunk,
And went inside to buy some more.
They only had little eight ounce bottles,
So instead of one, I bought four.

Chapter Nineteen

Anyway, it all ended well,
I also found some more brake fluid in back.
So the reservoir was filled to the brim,
After that we got more gas and a snack.
June was still a little concerned about the brakes.
She said she didn't like it when they went away.
"Don't worry," I said, "I'll check them more often."
So after lunch we were back on our way.

June was amazed when we passed Plymouth Rock.
She said she never believed there really was one.
I told her we could stop there some other time,
But right now I just wanted the trip to be done.
It was getting late when we arrived at Aunt Honey's.
Down the tree-lined drive stood the big house on a rise.
Behind it the ocean shined in the setting sun.
It was pretty, and June could hardly believe her eyes.

"This is your Aunt Honey's house?" She gasped.
"It looks like a mansion to me!"
I said it probably was,
And pretty soon she'd get to see.
We had stopped a few miles before
So June could get all gussied up for her interrogation.
She changed into a preppy angel right there while I watched,
Proper, but very hot and that's no exaggeration.

But now that she saw the house and the grounds,
She started feeling a little nervous inside.
She must have said "oh" a dozen times in a minute.
I was getting nervous now too, but I tried to look dignified.
We stopped in the circular driveway,
Right in front of the big double door.
It was quiet there after I shut off the car.
We could hear the waves splashing the shore.

I was helping June get out of the car,
When from behind me I heard Aunt Honey yell.
"Oh Donnie, Donnie, I'm so glad you're here."
It seemed like she meant it too, as far as I could tell.
She welcomed me with a crushing hug,
And a big wet kiss on my cheek.
She had put on quite a few pounds,
But I didn't mention it when I started to speak.

"Aunt Honey, this is June," I announced,
I was closely watching Aunt Honey's eyes,
Looking for any sign of disapproval.
But there wasn't any, to my surprise.
She gave June a big hug just like mine,
Said she was so glad to meet her.
Then added how very lovely she looked.
And like that, my stress disappeared in a blur.

Aunt Honey was seeing what I saw in June,
And June shined like a goddess divine.
We brought in the few things we had from the car,
June's wardrobe and a gym bag of mine.
Aunt Honey was clucking like a happy old hen,
She seemed really glad to see both of us.
I was expecting to see Uncle Ed too,
Because of all the noise and the fuss.

But it seemed we had the whole place to ourselves,
Cause Uncle Ed was fishing at the camp again.
Aunt Honey told me this later when I asked her,
But she made fishing sound like a sin.
I didn't think too much about it at the time,
There were so many other things to talk about,
But later she told me privately out back,
"Uncle Ed spends a lot of time with trout."

So naturally something smelled kind of fishy.
The camp was three or four hours away,
And wasn't there an ocean of fish right here,
So why would he drive for half a day?
Aunt Honey said the camp was nice and had a pond.
Ed told her he needed some place to get away.
The manager knew how to run the store,
But he would call him all the time anyway.

Aunt Honey and June hit it off really well,
Right from the very beginning.
I think it was because she looked so damn marvelous.
None of us could stop grinning.
June's soft southern drawl
Sounded so silky and sweet.
The two of them were chattering like mag-pies,
So I just watched from my seat.

June was asking lots of questions too.
It was a wonderful surprise.
I thought I would have to do all the talking,
And trying to avoid telling lies.
Then Aunt Honey started giving us the house tour,
Leading us down the halls.
She would point out all of the family and friends;
She had framed them on all the walls.

Mostly they were family pictures though,
A whole bunch were of her and Ed.
She beamed as she showed their wedding picture,
Then she giggled about a feather bed.
There were some pictures of the camp too
Where Uncle Ed spent so many of his days.
But when she pointed these out to us,
Ed didn't get as much praise.

Of course I had seen the house before,
But this time it seemed more forlorn.
Like a castle, big, cold, and lonely,
With carpets that were hardly worn.
I watched Aunt Honey
As she waddled from room to room.
Even though her voice was bright and cheery,
There was were signs of gloom.

The big house was really beautiful,
But sterile as an old clam shell.
They had never had any children,
Just big cars and lots of clientele.
Uncle Ed had a knack for making money.
He'd made a ton of it selling all those new cars.
And the dealership was growing bigger every year,
But instead of the satisfaction of success, he started going to the
    bars.

He'd never been a drinker,
But he'd quickly changed his tastes.
From coffee to rye and ginger,
Not that he was always strait-laced.
He had been known to have a beer or two,
But now he only drank the hard stuff,
And he couldn't stop at one or two,
With whiskey there was never enough.

I was sorry to hear this about my Uncle Ed,
He had always been very nice to me.
There had to be more to it though,
I could almost guarantee.
Something else was in the mix,
Besides what met the eye.
You don't just start drinking for no good reason,
So I had to find out why.

I changed the subject with Aunt Honey,
I didn't want to upset her more.
The girls made a great dish for supper
Right after the property tour.
It really tasted good and hearty, a lot better
Than the road food we had eaten on the fly.
It was quite a treat to sit down and relax,
And not worry about things like e-coli.

We talked and talked after dinner over wine,
Until it got to be pretty late.
There was so much to talk about,
And some of it couldn't wait.
Everyone was having a good time though.
I could tell Aunt Honey was bonding to June.
Cause they talked a lot about girl stuff and more,
And I started imagining our honeymoon.

I had worried that things wouldn't go this smoothly,
With Aunt Honey and our situation.
But it couldn't have been easier getting along,
It was more like a family vacation.
After eleven we broke up the party,
Aunt Honey showed us to our rooms upstairs.
We each had a private bath with tons of room,
But we stayed in my room, Auntie was unawares.

Tuesday

June really liked Cape Cod and the beach.
She had never seen the ocean before.
And now that she had she loved it.
There's something romantic about the shore,
It makes you realize that there is always change,
And nothing ever stays the same.
Everything's moving all the time,
And there's very little time for shame.

It was like paradise,
Having June with me there that way.
For over a week now we had been together,
Every minute of every day.
I was growing so in love with her,
What would I do if she should stray?
Every night she left me so breathless,
I'd be lost if she went away.

She knew I loved her,
Cause I told her every time I could.
And she was starting to hope, I think,
That she was into something good.
I wanted her to realize
I was that guy she'd never found.
And when she realized that,
We'd be wedding bound.

Of course Aunt Honey didn't have a clue
About how seriously I was in love.
Nor did my parents or even June realize,
What had descended on me from above.
But if this thing worked out, well then,
All of my fantasies would come true.
These fantasies were just optimistic dreams,
But they grew, and they grew, and they grew.

June and I were both starting to relax,
Aunt Honey was the perfect hostess.
She loved having company around,
I think we helped her loneliness.
Of course she was still the same old Aunt Honey,
And everything had to be done just right.
When she saw the oil stains from my car,
She ordered it behind the garage, out of sight.

That actually worked out just fine for us,
It became our little hidden love nest.
It was filled with memories of finding each other.
Most afternoons we'd be there undressed,
And snuggled under the U Haul blanket,
Loving the afternoon away.
When we returned from our "long walk" tired,
I'd bring Aunt Honey a forest bouquet.

That evening Uncle Ed came home,
He seemed glad to see us.
But everyone could smell the booze on his breath,
Although nobody made a fuss.
He gave us all a great big hug,
And chattered on like a tipsy magpie.
His stories were funny like in the old days,
But sometimes they didn't quite fly.

I noticed every once in a while,
Aunt Honey sat back in her chair,
As Eddie rambled on with his silly stories
Aunt Honey's mind was elsewhere.
She didn't have that old twinkle in her eye
That I remembered from years gone by.
But June enjoyed Eddie going on with his tales,
And there was a lot of twinkling in her eye.

That night as I was creeping past Auntie's door,
On my way to June's room down the hall,
I heard angry words being spoken inside.
They were loud but it wasn't a brawl.
When I didn't hear my name come up,
I continued down the hall toward my lover.
We could hear them arguing from there too,
But not as much after we went under cover.

Wednesday

Uncle Ed had left before breakfast in the morning,
He'd gone down to the dealership at first light.
Auntie said he had things to catch up on,
Since he hadn't been there since Friday night.
This was Wednesday, so he had to be a bit behind.
He'd been going to camp lately every weekend
And staying there three or four days.
Liking fishing that much is hard to comprehend.

I changed the subject and we talked about the sea.
June and I had planned to catch some sun,
I asked Aunt Honey if she wanted to come along,
But she said she had to go out and meet someone.
"But I'll just be a little while Donnie,
I'm sure y'all can get along out there fine without me."
And we did; the water was cold and the sun was hot,
But June and I found a perfect spot in the woods by the sea.

In the afternoon when Aunt Honey came back,
I told her June and I were going to see Uncle Ed and the lot,
June wanted to see the dealer ship and tour around.
I wanted to see the cars and maybe even his yacht.
But my battery was dead and there was no charger.
Aunt Honey said that was probably just fine,
Then she threw me her car key.
"Here Donnie," she said, "Take mine."

Chapter Twenty

Now there's a world of difference
Between a brand new car and mine.
This one had a radio, brakes, and a quiet exhaust,
And a nicer smell that wasn't canine.
We felt like millionaires going to town in Auntie's beautiful car.
It was shined up so much it sparkled in the sun.
There's just no comparison between new and used.
It started me thinking then, how could I get one?

The dealership had grown even bigger
Than I had remembered from years in the past.
It seemed like there were acres of cars,
And different brands too, the place was vast.
I was glad to be driving Aunt Honey's car there,
Showing up in my car would have been a joke.
It would've stuck out like the biggest sore thumb,
And that wouldn't include the dripping oil or the smoke.

Uncle Ed was in his office,
He jumped up right away when we walked in.
"Hey, great to see the both of you,
I'm glad you came right in."
"This place is so much bigger," I said,
"Than I remembered from years ago."
"Yeah Donnie, business has been good.
Real good! Things are never slow."

Then a beautiful brunette walked into the room.
She handed my Uncle some papers and turned to go,
But Ed grabbed her hand almost like he owned it.
He said to her, "Hey, Monica, whoa.
I want you to meet my nephew Donnie,
And his friend June from Tennessee."
She smiled and reached out her hand,
"Hello. Can I get you some coffee or tea?"

"Folks, this is Monica, my new secretary,
I don't know what I'd do without her.
She takes care of everything that comes up."
Then he paused and grinned like a fox at her.
Monica took our orders with a luscious smile.
"I'll be right back," Then she headed for the door.
I could hardly believe how sharp and sexy she was,
With her short skirt, heels, and all that curvature.

Uncle Ed noticed that I was noticing
His fabulously gorgeous secretary.
"Monica's been a big asset," he said.
"A really big help to me.
She only started about a year ago,
As an intern with my old secretary Pearl,
But after all those years she just up and quit one day.
And left everything here in a swirl."

"Well, Monica stepped right into the breach.
It was amazing all the things she got done.
And she's a lot faster than Pearl was,
Makes working here almost fun."
Uncle Ed was still talking about Monica
When she returned with our drinks on a tray.
Ed noticed she only brought three cups in.
"Get one for yourself" he said, "And stay."

Uncle Ed was in good form,
Smiling from ear to ear.
Monica was professional but very friendly,
Gorgeous and full of cheer.
We had a nice chat for nearly half an hour,
Then Uncle showed us around the showroom floor.
I could hardly believe there were so many cars.
And out back there were hundreds more!

We excused ourselves after the tour
To let Unc. get back to making money.
June and I took the long way home exploring
But I kept thinking about Aunt Honey.
June had been nearly overwhelmed
By Uncle Ed, Monica and all those cars.
"They are impressive," I said,
"But none of them are as nice as ours."

It was always a joy to see June laugh,
She thought that I was pretty funny.
I was laughing too on the outside,
But inside I needed money.
Cause once you see how the other half lives,
Something just clicks inside.
It hurts to not be the same as them,
And to drive a car that they make you hide.

"Wow, your uncle's secretary is really pretty,"
After we were back in the car alone.
I knew this was going to come up for discussion,
It was a thought you couldn't postpone.
"Yeah, you're right June.
Unc's got himself in quite a situation.
But I think there's more going on
Than coffee and a little dictation."

"I was thinking that too."
Said June, kind of smiling.
"She's beautiful and she's smart."
Then I added, "And beguiling too."
"Maybe," said June.
"But she really seems to know her job though."
I chuckled, "She's doing a lot of jobs June,
Most of them are on Uncle Ed, you know?"

June understood what I was saying,
"Yeah, you might be right.
But do you think they're having an affair?
And not just some little office delight?"
"I don't see a lot of difference there June.
Either way Aunt Honey's getting screwed.
I think she already suspects something's not right.
I have to find the truth even if I have to intrude."

"You know June, Auntie's put on a lot of weight.
She used to be almost as thin as you just last year.
She'll be 200 soon at this rate!
Most guys don't like to see that much extra gear."
"I guess not Don. Your Aunt is pretty heavy.
I'm wondering which came first, it's hard to tell,
Was it Monica or the weight?"
"It doesn't matter June, Monica has cast her spell."

"This is terrible Don.
What are we going to do?"
"I don't know," I said and I meant it too.
"We have to be careful whatever we do.
I think we have to make darn sure
Before we point any fingers."
"You're right about that June," I said.
"Fallout from this kind of thing always lingers."

I made up my mind to have a heart to heart talk
Real soon with Uncle Ed.
We needed to know the truth
Before anything else was said.
I needed to find a way
To talk to him all alone.
I thought of calling him up,
But you never get anything done on the phone.

On our way back to the house,
I bought June a big ice cream cone.
She was getting used to all my words of love by now.
I even told her that all my wild oats had been sown.
She smiled cause she liked to hear me talk like that,
But then she wrinkled up her pretty brow,
"But Don, I like the oats you sow.
I hope you're not going to run out now."

I assured her all I had were hers,
No one else would get anymore.
She was my love and I was her guy.
Hers alone right to the core.
She drank up my words of affection.
Despite her ordeals she had a very warm heart,
She wanted to believe what I was saying to her
Every time I called her "sweetheart."

I was beginning to feel fairly certain
That she had started to love me too.
And not just because of our nightly behavior,
At our secret rendezvous.
Every night after Aunt Honey went to sleep,
We were making a deeper connection.
I could feel my love growing bigger every day,
And I'm not just talking about my erection.

Also Aunt Honey was different now too,
The old religion had cooled from what it'd been.
But she still had her Bible by her chair,
And went to church and talked about sin.
She even quoted a little scripture,
Every now and then,
But the fires of un-forgiveness had cooled down,
And for that we could all say, "Amen."

Because now she had grown more affectionate,
More than she had ever been before.
And she really seemed to care about us,
Always smiling and trying to do more.
The longer we stayed with her,
The more I became really sure
I didn't want her getting hurt
By Uncle Ed and his beautiful whore.

Of course, I was jumping to conclusions,
I really knew nothing for sure.
I needed to confront Uncle Ed
And try to find out some more.
That evening after supper we had cigars
And took a walk down by the shore.
I mentioned something about his new camp,
And hoped he'd tell me more.

He lit up in excitement
At just the sound of the place.
He said he was going up there this weekend
To get a little breathing space.
Then he invited me and June to come along,
Said we really ought to give it a go.
I knew June would be willing,
And I just couldn't say no.

June indeed was excited about going up to Maine,
When I told her about it later that night.
But Aunt Honey had an excuse for not going,
Which didn't seem to me quite right.
She said she'd be just fine
Staying at home all by herself.
She planned on going to church on Sunday.
On Saturday she was working at the food shelf.

Chapter Twenty One

Thursday

In the am. Unc. asked me to go with him to the lot.
June and Auntie were going shopping in town.
I thought this might be the chance I needed,
To ask about Monica, and really pin him down.
But he was so friendly as we drove to town,
There was no way I could bring it up then.
It was kind of fun hanging out with Uncle Ed,
And it wasn't hard looking at Monica again.

She was dazzling in black and white,
Sharp and friendly and oh so charming,
Even more than the day before.
But it was her perfume that was most disarming.
She brought in coffee right away,
Then fussed over us for a minute or two.
After that she brought Unc up to speed with the business,
All the items, both the old and the new.

After she left and had closed the door,
Unc turned to me and said,
"Isn't she amazing Donnie?
Ya gotta admit it, go ahead!"
"You're right about that Uncle Ed.
She's the finest secretary I've ever seen."
Unc started laughing, "I think so too," he said.
But he made it sound kind of obscene.

Before I could bring up any of my thoughts about her,
Uncle Ed sat down and got really serious,.
"Donnie, I've got a proposition for you to consider.
It could be a good thing for both of us.
As you can see, this is a big operation here.
But I'm not sure everybody's playing fair.
I don't suspect anybody right now of cheating me,
But it's happened before and I need to be aware."

"I need somebody I can trust around here.
Somebody that's blood like you.
You're in the family, one of us.
How'd you like to join the crew?
It's not like I'm paranoid or something's wrong,
It's not that I can't trust anyone here,
Cause I do. I trust them all a lot,
Not quite a hundred percent, but near."

"I'm offering you a job, Donnie.
I need another set of eyes and ears.
Someone who can watch my back, you know.
Keep a lookout for the racketeers,
Or anybody else that's trying to rip me off.
You'd be surprised at all the tricks there are.
I'll teach you so you can spot them all.
Some of them are really bizarre."

"Everything from stealing car parts and oil,
And siphoning off gasoline,
To changing invoices, or time sheets,
Or even robbing the vending machine."
"Uncle Ed, I don't have any experience for this," I said.
"I wouldn't know where to start, I don't have a clue."
"Donnie, Donnie, please, just call me Ed down here.
Only Monica knows you're my nephew."

I was dumbfounded, but proud,
That Unc would offer me such a position,
But I didn't know a thing about the car business.
I didn't think I could make the transition.
"Don't worry about that Donnie.
You'll get the hang of it all right away."
"Well, what exactly would I be doing Ed?
And how much is it going to pay?"

"I'll pay you twenty per cent more than you're getting now."
I still didn't think I was cut out to be a spy.
He could see I was not convinced, "How about twenty five?"
"I don't know Ed, I don't think I'm your guy."
"Donnie, please, you'd be doing me a big favor."
I was starting to give in.
Family was important to me too after all,
And his offer seemed genuine.

But money was an important consideration too.
"I don't know Ed, I'd like to help you out.
But I'm not making all that much in Memphis,
And living up here, well, I'd be down and out."
Uncle Ed asked me what I was making in Memphis,
And when I told him he slapped his head.
"You're right!
I better double that," he said.

I could hardly believe my Uncle was a car salesman.
He had to be the worst one I ever knew.
Car dealers are supposed to skin you alive,
Not him, and there was more he was going to do.
"And Donnie, it's not just the pay check every week.
There'll be lots of perks included too.
You'll get health insurance and year-end bonuses,
And a car to drive that's new."

Now he had hit my softest spot,
A new car was worth more to me than pay.
"Really? What kind?" I eagerly asked.
"Doesn't matter, you can pick one out today.
I've got a batch of demos you can drive.
Pick one out or drive a different one every day.
I sell them off when they get a few miles.
Keeps the inventory fresh that way."

I was overwhelmed with all the talk of money and cars,
But I had to digest the idea a little more.
"That sounds great Uncle Ed," I told him.
"And everything tells me to say, 'OK, sure,'
But it's such a big change that I wasn't expecting.
Can I think about it a bit?"
"Of course Donnie. Take your time of course.
I don't want you to start and then quit."

I knew I was going to have to take this deal,
It was just too good to be true.
But I wanted to talk it over with June,
And see if she liked it too.
We'd have to get an apartment,
Not too fancy but something nearby.
I thought she would like it on the Cape,
But would she want to be the wife of a spy?

My head was spinning,
There was so much going on inside.
Offers like this don't come along every day,
But at least I had some time to decide.
I figured I better ask more questions,
Try to get a handle on what I'd be doing.
"So Ed, how exactly would we approach this thing?
I'm still not sure where this is going."

Uncle Ed smiled real big,
In a slightly mischievous way.
"I've been thinking about this part for quite a while.
And this is where you'll earn your pay.
You'll have to be completely undercover.
So no one suspects you're related to me.
You'll be the new kid from out of town.
A little down on his luck, like a refugee."

"You'll start out at the bottom.
Down in the shop sweeping the floors.
But you'll be making the same as my top mechanics.
Just doing menial chores.
That way, everybody will trust you.
They won't have anything worth hiding.
You'll be just like one of them.
I want to know who's working and who's riding."

"Not a bad idea Uncle Ed,
But I don't know how long I can play that role,
Eventually the truth will leak out.
And I'll look like a big asshole.
And I wouldn't have any friends either, you know."
"You shouldn't be friends with thieves or worse!
Remember, you're on the right side of the law,
They're the ones perverse!"

"It all depends on how well you play your role Donnie.
If you're good at it you could go on forever.
Everything would be discrete on my end.
You can do it son. You just have to be clever.
And if your cover does get blown Donnie,
It doesn't mean you'd be out in the cold.
By then you'd know how things run around here,
You're family Donnie, you can stay here till you're old."

The whole thing sounded pretty plausible,
The way Uncle Ed described it to me.
When he said he had a car for me,
How could I disagree?
We'll fix your car so you can drive it to work.
It will be part of your cover,
Then you can have a new one for personal use.
No one will ever discover,

"But Uncle Ed," I said,
You mean I'm going to have two cars?"
"You are Donnie. How about one of these?"
He was pointing to a row of Jaguars.
"There nice," I said.
"But that's a little too fancy for me.
"Can't I have a pickup truck instead?
It would go with the cowboy hat I got for free."

Uncle Ed just shook his head and smiled,
"So you want a truck instead of a fine car?
What's the world coming to now a days?
Ok, forget the Jaguar.
Let's go over there and pick one out."
"Well, ah Ed, we don't really have a deal yet.
I still want to talk it over with June."
"I understand Donnie. In that case take this Vette."

"I think that will help her decide
That you should come and work for your Uncle Ed."
Finally I was beginning to get used to the idea,
The money, the truck and everything that he said.
I drove the Corvette back to the house,
What an improvement over my old clunker!
I wasn't used to having everything working.
It was a rocket ship compared to my old junker!

Chapter Twenty Two

June and Aunt Honey weren't back from shopping yet,
And I wished that they had been.
I had so many thoughts swirling in my mind,
I was in a situation I had never been in.
Usually everything is going wrong,
And I have to figure out how to fix it.
This time everything was going right,
And I didn't want to jinx it.

I went out behind the garage,
And sat behind the wheel of my old car.
I had made a lot of decisions from this seat
That had taken me pretty far.
I was hoping the old girl had one more good idea left.
But thinking is about the hardest work you can do,
Especially when it's about the future,
And you never have a clue.

Or maybe it was just all so new,
A total change from what I'd known.
Always before I was fixing things up,
Patching them up after they'd blown.
That was the kind of predicaments
I was used to dealing with every day.
I was used to my life falling apart,
Now everything was coming my way.

I felt like I had just won the lottery,
Like every dream had come true.
I wasn't prepared for so much good fortune,
I really didn't know what to do.
Sometimes the good can be as vexing as the bad,
But at least with the bad I could usually repair it.
With the good I'd have to be more careful,
Cause with my luck I'd probably impair it.

Was this some kind of stupid,
Feeling sorry for myself because of a good break?
I had to smile as I looked around the inside of my car.
It looked like it'd been in an earthquake.
What the hell was I worried about? I reasoned.
There was no place to go but up from this mess.
I was impatient for June to get home to tell her,
We were no longer going to get by with less.

And that was another thing that surprised me too.
Auntie and June were like mother and daughter,
Out shopping like they'd done it all their lives.
Instead of preaching hell fire, and slaughter,
Aunt Honey was being the perfect hostess,
Gracious, gentle, trusting and kind.
Not that I missed the Old Testament war wagon,
But I thought it couldn't be too far behind.

Once she got a few of the unholy details,
Of our hasty and carnal relationship,
I could expect the strongest of condemnations,
And that would be the end of our fellowship.
It was bound to happen,
The truth always comes out.
Of course sooner would be worse than later.
As barracuda is to trout.

And if all of this history came into the light,
Would everything be blown sky high?
What would become of my new spy job,
And what about June and I?
So much speculation was giving me a headache,
I don't think I was cut out to fret.
Things were a lot simpler before this came up,
And if it all fell apart, they would be yet.

Finally they rolled up the driveway,
And I was lifted from my worrying trance.
They seemed like two little girls,
Chattering like teenagers just home from the dance.
I was so glad to see June again,
And anxious to tell her about the new deal.
She was happy about her new high heel boots,
With all the fancy leather and practically a steal.

She really did look good in them too,
With the frilly white blouse and the jeans tucked in.
I complimented her and pointed to the Vette.
"Would you like to take a spin?"
She was enchanted.
We told Aunt Honey we'd be back real soon,
But she said, "Take your time, just be careful."
"You've got the whole afternoon."

It was the nicest afternoon behind the wheel.
I felt like a king in that Corvette,
And June looked like my radiant queen,
Even though we weren't quite married yet.
I told her all about the job I was offered,
And all the perks about being a spy.
She was enthusiastic and said,
"Go for it Don. You've got to give it a try!"

I reminded her how much I loved her and said,
I wouldn't do anything that she wasn't for.
I wanted us to be together as one,
Whether it was for richer or poor.
She was not ready for anything that formal yet,
But she agreed we should get our own place.
I was so happy I had to stop the car,
Just to hold her in a loving embrace.

For guys, feeling successful is a real turn on,
And that went the same for her.
So after a few minutes of hugging and smooching,
We both were starting to purr.
But there's no back seat in those little Corvettes,
Nor did we have our U Haul blanket close by,
But there was a Ramada Inn on the road up ahead.
I suggested we give it a try.

June and I were of one mind in this decision,
We looked a little fishy without a suitcase,
But we really didn't care and neither did they,
All we needed was a little private space.
Hotels were becoming one of our favorite places,
I don't even remember what I paid.
But the room was nice, had a comfy bed,
But June was the reason I stayed.

These loving moments with her,
Were just getting better each time.
Whenever I thought they couldn't improve,
Some new song would begin to rhyme.
We went from jazz to pop to a symphony,
Enjoying every note and every key,
And we both heard the music together,
It wasn't only just me.

Before we checked out and went back to Auntie's,
I explained more about my new job to June.
She was amazed at the pay and all of the perks,
And that we'd have our own place real soon.
Cause I couldn't keep creeping down the hallways,
Just to get into her bed.
But we wondered what Aunt Honey would say,
When we rented a place unwed?

We all had supper together for a change,
Uncle Ed got home before we ate.
I thanked him for the job as we sat around the table,
And asked him if he had a starting date?
He was grinning and I noticed a chuckle,
As he pondered the best way to bring me in.
"Donnie, that's great," he finally said,
"Next week's a fine time to begin."

And just like that,

I had the best job I ever had.

June and I were overflowing with thanks.

Everyone was happy and glad.

We all went to bed early that night,

So we could rest up for the big weekend.

I was too tired to slip down the hall,

But I was sure June would still be my friend.

Chapter Twenty Three

Friday

The next morning Ed left early to go down to the lot,
While June or I were still in the sack.
I figured he had a lot to do before he could leave,
Things that couldn't wait until he got back.
Aunt Honey made a delicious breakfast for us,
That filled me up to the brim.
Then we took a walk on the beach,
But I was too full to swim.

We had a leisurely morning,
Walking along the shore.
What a different person I seemed to be,
I didn't feel like a kid anymore.
My life had improved so much and so fast,
And it wasn't just my new job with Ed.
It was more internal and deep,
I was imagining June and I wed.

We parked the Vette at the lot,
Just a minute or two before noon.
Promptly at noon Uncle Ed appeared at the door,
And motioned toward me and June.
He wanted us to get into the SUV
That he was driving up to Maine,
But there was Monica sitting in the front seat.
Suddenly everything was getting insane.

"I should have mentioned about Monica coming."
Uncle Ed apologized with a stupid grin.
"She's coming with us for a few days," he said.
"Hi," she chirped behind the sunglasses as June and I climbed in.
Neither of us could think of anything to say,
At least for a second or two.
Then finally June spoke up and said with a smile,
"Monica, how nice it is to see you."

And we were off to the woods of Maine.
I still couldn't think of anything to say,
Except "Yeah," and then "Great,"
But neither word came out the right way.
The car was pretty quiet after that;
June and I were so dumbfounded.
Monica and Ed were chatting away,
And I didn't like the way it sounded.

It was obvious in a heartbeat
That all of my suspicions were true.
They were having a secret affair;
Apparently nobody had a clue.
I thought of Aunt Honey sitting at home all alone,
Not knowing of her Eddie's affair.
I didn't know what to say or do about it,
And Eddie didn't seem to care.

Of course I had a lot of questions too,
Welling up inside of my head.
But they would have to wait a while,
Till I had some private time with Ed.
On the other hand June finally found her voice,
And she and Monica started talking away.
Ed would pipe in every once in a while with a comment,
But I didn't have much to say.

Monica was such a beautiful charmer,
She couldn't have been sweeter if she tried.
Vivacious, witty, sexy and smart,
If I said I didn't like her then I lied.
By the time we got through the Boston traffic,
She had all of us laughing like kids.
It almost made me forget for a moment
That Ed's marriage was on the skids.

June and Monica fit together like two long lost sisters,
It was really fun to see.
Monica brought out a funny side of June
That was spontaneous and completely carefree.
Monica really did make the trip something to enjoy
Cause Uncle Ed and I weren't quite so chatty.
The girls turned the long ride into a hilarious trip,
Otherwise I might have gone batty.

We stopped at a nice restaurant for dinner,
And Eddie picked up the tab.
He said it'd be easier that making supper at camp,
Then he recommended the lobster or the crab.
We all went with lobster
And the girls had a few glasses of wine.
Ed had four bourbons and tossed me his keys.
I just had a beer and was fine.

I guess it all would have been perfect
If I could have gotten Aunt Honey out of my mind.
But deep down I knew it just wasn't right,
In fact it was downright unkind.
If Ed had any feelings about what he was doing,
He was drinking them all away.
Nor was Monica troubled with guilt;
Like Ed, she was just as blasé.

I saw Ed motion to the waitress,
He wanted to have one more bourbon to drink.
About then Monica's hand slipped under the table,
And she gave him an unsubtle wink.
"You've got some work to do tonight mister.
I don't want you going to sleep on the job."
Unc quickly waved the waitress on by.
I could almost hear his horny heart throb.

Monica and Ed got into the back seat,
As I drove the rest of the way to camp.
They were warming up for a festive evening.
A couple of times Monica even called him "Champ."
June and I smiled at each other,
We didn't need warmed up a degree.
It wasn't far to Eddie's camp,
And I was as ready as I ever would be.

The "camp'" was more like a nice new house;
There wasn't anything primitive about it.
But Ed called it a camp whenever he spoke,
So I had no reason to doubt it.
It was obvious Monica had been there before.
She pointed out their room at the end of the hall.
And then our room with its own bathroom,
Then excused herself to go with Ed, who smiled and said, "Have a
    ball."

The camp reminded us of a hotel room in the woods,
And we lost no time enjoying it and the quiet night.
Eventually June fell asleep in my arms exhausted,
But I laid awake still uptight.
Maybe Puritan ghosts hovering around the room,
Putting churchy thoughts into my head.
But whoever was throwing those thoughts at me,
They all rolled back to Ed.

I couldn't get past him having an affair,
Though I had suspected it for days on end.
Maybe it was his "so what" attitude toward Auntie
That made it so hard to defend.
I could understand his attraction to Monica,
She was beautiful right to the bone,
But looking and touching were two different things.
But then, who was I to throw a stone?

Anyway, it troubled me,
And I knew it couldn't be hidden forever.
Sooner or later there would be an explosion,
I just didn't want to be the one to pull that lever.
Finally I did fall asleep,
But I was restless and had a lot of bad dreams.
I was trying to herd chickens into their coop,
But they wouldn't respond to my screams.

I wasn't feeling all that great.
When I got up a little late the next day,
The girls were up and had been out and back
With coffee and a bakery display.
Bagels and cream puffs, donuts and drinks,
A breakfast feast I was certainly ready for.
As I reached for a donut I looked for Ed,
And that's when I heard him snore.

He didn't get up until after ten.
By then we had gone out to fish.
Maybe it was the bourbon that did him in,
Or maybe Monica granted his every wish.
But when he first got up that morning
He was looking pretty old and tired,
Till Monica fed him a lot of coffee and donuts,
And pretty soon he was all re-wired.

We cooked the trout we caught in the morning.
They made a really delicious meal.
I was starting to feel a little more comfortable,
But it still was a pretty strange deal.
Monica was a lot of fun to be around,
And she and June got along quite well.
I still wanted things to work out with Auntie and Ed,
But he seemed more attracted to Jezebel.

I knew Uncle Ed was feeling better after lunch,
Cause he opened another bottle of booze.
We all had a drink and were feeling pretty good.
When Ed said, "Hey, let's retire and take a snooze.
Just a little short quiet afternoon nap,
It'll make us all feel better," he declared.
He asked the girls what they thought of the idea,
But neither of them really cared.

It seemed that no one was as eager as Uncle Ed
To get back in bed in the middle of the day.
"Ok!" he said, as if we had all agreed with him.
"This time let's do it a different way.
Let's change partners this time around.
Monica, you go down to Donnie's room with him,
And June, you can lay down with me.
Then later we'll all go for a swim."

I couldn't believe my ears,
And I know June was truly amazed,
But Monica just smiled happily
And looked towards me unfazed.
"Are you shitting me?"
I yelled at Ed.
I didn't care if my job was lost.
He was going to hear everything that I said.

Cause everything in my head came loose,
I accused him of cheating on poor Aunt Honey,
And I didn't cut him an inch of slack.
I didn't care anymore about my job or his money.
If he thought he was going to sleep with my June,
It'd be over my dead body.
I grabbed June's hand and we went outside,
"Ed," I yelled, "Pour yourself another totty."

I was burning up over Uncle Ed's suggestion,
Totally filled with anger and disgust.
He thought he could do whatever he wanted just because of his
    money,
And everyone else could adjust.
June and I went for a long walk in the woods.
I was so mad I thought I would bust.
Nothing mattered to Uncle Ed,
Just his money and his selfish lust.

June was wonderful to let me talk it out,
Even though it took me quite a while.
Finally I got myself calmed down,
But I knew Ed and I could never reconcile.
As soon as we got back to camp,
We would pack up all of our stuff,
Go to the Cape and head out of town.
We both agreed, enough was enough.

I didn't know where we would go,
But it didn't much matter to me.
If I had June beside me all the while,
We'd find some way through the debris.
What a relief it was to get all of this off my chest,
Now June was more precious to me than before.
She was someone who would stay and listen to me.
That made me want her all the more.

We embraced and kissed each other
Until we could no longer stand.
So onto the soft green grass we laid down
In a lover's wonderland.
I felt there was nothing I could buy,
Or any wealth I could have ever found,
That could make me as happy in life,
As laying there with June on the ground.

We talked afterwards,
And tenderly made our plans.
We'd tell Ed to take us back to the Cape
And out of these frying pans.
He could shove his job,
And all his spying games,
Cause we weren't going to have any part.
Of him going down in flames.

It was getting late by now
As we started to walk back to the camp.
It was time to tell Ed and Monica the news.
And I hoped there wouldn't be a fight.
The sun had already gone down,
As we reached the far edge of the pond.
Just then we heard a loud noise by the camp,
Or maybe it was just beyond.

When it happened a second time,
And it came to me in an instant.
It was the sound of a gun going off,
And we wondered what it meant.
As we ran around the pond toward the camp,
I could see the problem from afar.
Right there in the driveway by the door was where
Aunt Honey had parked her car.

The Trip: A Modern Odyssey

Chapter Twenty Four

We ran up to the front door,
Which was opened a little bit.
Aunt Honey was standing just inside
With a shotgun and having a fit.
Unc and Monica had their hands way up in the air,
Over against the bedroom wall.
Apparently Auntie had caught them red handed,
Cause they weren't wearing much at all.

She was holding Ed's twelve gauge shotgun,
And smoke was still coming out of the end.
This gun I knew could hold seven rounds,
Which meant she had five more to expend.
It wasn't hard to know the frame of her mind,
As she racked another shot in the chamber.
She had more than enough ammo to do us all in,
And in the heat of the moment who could blame her.

Auntie was so mad at Monica and Ed,
She was yelling words I didn't think she knew
And crying and wiping the tears away.
There was no way to tell what she'd do.
I could see two big holes in the wall,
Just above the culprits' heads.
I figured the next shot that was coming
Was going to be aimed at Ed's.

And he knew it too.
So he was talking really, really fast.
He used every pitch he had in his sales book,
Cause he knew his next words could be his last.
I knew I better step in real soon,
And I did just as Auntie finally told him to shut up.
"Aunt Honey," I said, calmly as I reached for the barrel,
"Please Aunt Honey, you've got to put the gun up."

"Donnie, that no good son of a bitch,
Has been cheating on me.
I caught them right there in the bed."
There was nothing I could do but agree.
"I ought to blow both their heads off,
They don't give a shit about me.
Eddie, you're just a two timing son of a bitch!"
Again I had to agree.

"But Auntie, you know it still ain't right.
To take the law into your own hands."
"Donnie, you know it'd be temporary insanity at the courthouse,
Without any 'ifs', or 'ands.'"
Again, I had to say, that that was probably true,
But that didn't make it alright.
"What about an eye for an eye?" she said.
"What about them screwing all night?"

"Auntie," I said again,
"You're not supposed to kill your husband,
Though you got a good reason to do it.
Maybe God won't understand?"
Now, at last, I had hit a nerve,
And she turned to answer me.
Uncle Ed was waiting for just such a moment,
And he took off like he was stung by a bee.

Monica dove for the floor at the same time,
And Auntie was caught by surprise.
So she instinctively pulled the trigger just then.
I felt the blast go right past my eyes.
Then she turned and took more careful aim,
By now Ed had gotten outside.
He was on the lawn streaking for the trees,
Desperate for a place to hide.

The next shot hit him right on his bare ass,
I know cause I heard him yell,
But by then he had gotten into the trees.
Despite the hit, he still was running really well.
But Auntie wasn't through with him yet,
Because she racked in another round.
The next shot took some leaves off the bushes
As Eddie dove for the ground.

Auntie kept shooting at him
As he ran on through the trees,
But she didn't get any more hits
Cause I could still hear him yelling "Please!"
I think she was just glad to keep him running.
It was a hell of a grand farewell.
Finally Auntie ran out of bullets,
And of course it was just as well.

"Keep running you son of a bitch!" she yelled.
Then she slumped onto the couch in tears.
June and I did our best to comfort her,
But she kept repeating, "All these years."
And, "That no good son of a bitch,
Cheating on me all these years."
Monica skedaddled back into the bedroom,
While Auntie was mopping her tears.

After a few minutes of crashing around it got quiet in there,
Then I heard the car start up outside.
Monica must have gone out the same window as Ed
When he was looking for a place to hide.
She probably picked him up on her way out,
As he was running down the drive.
I don't know if she brought him clothes to wear,
But either way he had to be glad to be alive.

We tried to get Aunt Honey calmed down.
June made us all hot cups of tea,
Then we offered Auntie some comforting words,
And tried to relax after her spree.
But every so often she couldn't say another word,
Before she cussed out Eddie to the n'th degree.
But June won her confidence whenever this happened,
Cause she would always agree.

I suggested we get our things together,
Lock up the place and head back.
I knew Aunt Honey would not want to spend the night
In Uncle Eddie's disgusting love shack.
In a way our road trip ended when
We pulled back into the drive
It was the middle of the night on the Cape,
But at least we were all still alive.

We helped Aunt Honey settle in for the night,
She was tired, hurt, angry and bitter.
But she took a couple of pills for sleeping that worked really well,
And by morning she decided Ed wasn't going to get her.
So after breakfast she called a shark-like attorney she knew,
She was determined to crucify Ed.
After she told him all the details at the camp and hung up,
She was delighted by what he had said.

We were all relieved to learn later on,
That Eddie's injuries weren't too serious,
We pictured Monica digging pellets out of his butt,
And laughed until we were delirious.
We heard that Ed missed a few days of work,
Cause he must have had a very sore ass,
But eventually it probably healed up
Or like the rest of him, it just turned into brass.

Epilogue

Five years later:

It's hard to know how trips will end
When you start out on them that first day.
You think you're headed to one place.
But things change along the way.
I guess in a way a trip never ends,
It just goes on forever and ever.
Even when you pass away,
It's only to a new endeavor.

Aunt Honey and Uncle Eddie,
Never re-united after the shooting,
In fact the marriage ended at the courthouse,
Where Eddie accused her of looting.
Cause she got the big house, lots of alimony,
And the car and the camp,
Plus all the money in the bank.
Eddie just got the bills and the tramp.

But Monica didn't stay with him very long,
Soon she found herself a rich attorney
Who was soon her newest best friend.
It wasn't long before she started a different journey.
Aunt Honey asked us to stay on with her for a while,
And help her adjust to her new life style.
Eventually we worked all the ruffles out,
But it wasn't without some strife for a while.

A big problem for her, I guess,
Was that June and I were sleeping in the same bed.
It went against her principles of religion and faith,
And I think it reminded her of Ed.
Anyway, she softened somewhat when I told her,
That I, at least, wanted us to get married.
So we had a lot of talks with June over the months,
And eventually the motion carried.

The preacher at her church
Married us on the beach in the spring.
My folks and June's Mom attended,
And then we went on our wedding fling,
We spent a week at the camp in Maine,
We hiked in the hills and fished in the pond,
And took a lot of walks in the woods,
Where I made love to my beautiful blond.

Aunt Honey eventually revived her religious fervor,
And for a while was a missionary overseas.
She told me I had to stay and take care of her house,
Otherwise I was free to do as I pleased.
I soon got a job as a carpenter's helper,
And June got a job at Walmart.
I fit right in with the crew,
And pretty soon I was learning the art.

In a couple of months I got a nice raise.
With that and all the help from Aunt Honey,
Like free rent and a car with insurance,
We were able to save a lot of money,
Which was just what we would be needing.
I wanted to build us a house of our own.
By the end of a year I was surprised to see
Just how much our savings had grown.

Uncle Ed stayed on with his dealership.
Once in a while we'd see him in a TV ad.
Otherwise we never saw him at all,
He still made all of us kind of mad.
But he's been regular with the alimony,
A big check comes each month when it should.
Aunt Honey has finally gotten over her hurts,
Though for a while there we didn't think she would.

But she has moved on since then,
And I think now she's a lot happier too.
She lost lots of pounds, bought some new clothes,
And has gotten a healthier view.
Ed stills drinks too much bourbon and water
And hasn't lost any of his weight.
He probably will someday, after he dies,
But by then it'll be too late.

After sitting behind the garage for a year,
I had my car towed to the local junk yard.
That car and I had gone a lot of miles together,
So taking her to the scrap yard was hard.
She had brought me to the end of my rainbow
Where I had found my pot of gold.
I had found my golden-haired lady,
To forever have and to hold.

But there's a souvenir of that memorable trip
That we keep tucked away in our chest.
And once in a while,
When we really feel blessed,
And the kids are sound asleep,
And nobody's likely to intrude,
We put that U-Haul blanket on the bed,
And in seconds our love is re-brewed.

And yes, I did mention kids,
A boy and a pair of twin girls.
Donald junior is two,
And April and May have all the curls.
There may be more coming someday too,
Cause we may not be done just yet.
June is quite a mother and a fabulous lover too,
And I'm just happy to take care of the debt.

There's a good chance I can do it too,
Cause now I'm the foreman with my own crew.
Got a big raise and perks and bonuses to boot.
Now I run the job and tell everybody else what to do.
So I don't think I'll be taking any more trips
For quite a long time to come,
Cause I'm enjoying the one I'm still on,
Doing anything else would be dumb.

The End

www.ingramcontent.com/pod-product-compliance
Lightning Source LLC
Chambersburg PA
CBHW071956040426
42447CB00009B/1356